All Hands Stand By to Repel Boarders

All Hands Stand By to Repel Boarders

Tales from Life as a Lutheran Pastor

Cordell Strug

RESOURCE *Publications* • Eugene, Oregon

ALL HANDS STAND BY TO REPEL BOARDERS
Tales from Life as a Lutheran Pastor

Copyright © 2013 Cordell Strug. All rights reserved. Except for brief quotations in critical publications or reviews, no part of this book may be reproduced in any manner without prior written permission from the publisher. Write: Permissions, Wipf and Stock Publishers, 199 W. 8th Ave., Suite 3, Eugene, OR 97401.

Resource Publications
An Imprint of Wipf and Stock Publishers
199 W. 8th Ave., Suite 3
Eugene, OR 97401
www.wipfandstock.com

ISBN 13: 978-1-62564-163-2

Manufactured in the U.S.A.

Scripture quotations, unless otherwise marked, are from the New Revised Standard Version Bible, Copyright © 1989 by the Division of Christian Education of the National Council of the Churches of Christ in the USA. Used by permission. All rights reserved.

To the pastors of the Evangelical Lutheran Church in America

I consider the days of old,
>   and remember the years of long ago.
I commune with my heart in the night;
>   I meditate and search my spirit . . .

—PSALM 77:5–6

All remembrance of things past is fiction . . .

—ERNEST HEMINGWAY, *A MOVEABLE FEAST (FRAGMENTS)*

 . . . I dare say I am a much more annoying
>   person than I know.

—C. S. LEWIS, *REFLECTIONS ON THE PSALMS*

Contents

Acknowledgments xi
Prologue: Tacit Knowledge xiii

Part One

All Hands Stand By to Repel Boarders 3

Caveat Lector 10

Extremely Isolated, Extremely Cold, Extremely Dark 14

Beating the Bounds 20

The Little Trailer on the Corner 24

What's a Nice Philosopher like You Doing in a Profession like This? 29

Holy Things 32

Hanging out 36

Saint Ken 39

Part Two

The Woman in the Window 47

Occupational Hazards 50

Visiting 52

The Visited 57

On the Road 61

Perspectives 67

At War with the (Christian) Family 68

The Queen of Hearts in paradise 72

Contents

The Great Thing 74

Looking Back on the Great Thing 80

My Desk, and What I Had There 82

Fearless Moral Inventories 84

Fred and Ginger 86

When the Dead Awaken 92

Of Little Faith (1) 94

Part Three

Required Reading 101

Breakdowns 102

People That Drove Me Nuts (1) 107

People That Drove Me nuts (2) 109

People That Drove Me Nuts (3) 113

People That Drove Me Nuts (4) 116

People That Drove Me Nuts (5) 122

The Church Heals the Help 124

Four Statements You Should Know How to Make 130

Part Four

Of Little Faith (2) 133

Role Models 136

Occupational Hazards (2): The Perils of Decency 139

The Iceberg 147

Why You Get Phone Calls in the Middle of the Night 152

Passing Through 154

Mother and Son at Christmas 163

(One of) My Worst Day(s) 167

Three of My Failures 170

Trying to Go On 175

Raging at the Dead 181

The Emptiest Word in the English Language 185

Part Five

Flesh 189

Breath 192

Sorrow 197

Fade out 200

Appendix to "Saint Ken" 205
Appendix to "Looking Back on the Great Thing" 211

Acknowledgments

SEVERAL PEOPLE DESERVE THANKS for agreeing to look at parts of this writing as it was taking shape, and for offering comments and suggestions: Fred Gaiser, Peter Geisendorfer-Lindgren, Gary and Ruth Halverson, Arland Hultgren, Arland Jacobson, Harold Lohr, Ken Losch, Mary Preus, Carrie and Robert Smith, Mary Carol Strug, Gary Taylor. Paul Sponheim and Rick Hest provided extensive commentary on each part. Above all, I must thank Sylvia Ruud, who saw the first fragments of this and saw what they might be. She urged them towards clarity, organization, and completion. She saw the possibilities for illustration and chose the photographs. This book would not have taken shape as it has without her.

Prologue: Tacit Knowledge

When I attended seminary, most of my teachers were ordained, but my New Testament Greek teacher was a layperson, Mary Preus. She had that radiant blend of beauty, brilliance, erudition, humor, and generosity that could renew your faith in life and human possibility, until you met the next dozen or so people. Then you knew what a rare gift she was to anyone who met her. I liked her a lot.

Since I was ten years older than most of my classmates, I tended to stand out a little. But I stood out more for Mrs. Preus, as we always called her with great respect, because I had taken three years of Latin at a Roman Catholic high school. So I picked up the Greek grammar easily and, at least as important, I got all of her jokes. There's a kind of humor, with a set of allusions, that flourishes among Latin students and Classics majors, which I despair of communicating to outsiders but which is instantly grasped within the fold.

It goes like this:

One year, I signed up for a seminar Mrs. Preus offered in Classical Greek. Obviously, only the highest of highflyers signed up for this. When she walked in and saw who we were, she smiled and said, "I should toss an apple on the table and say 'This is for the smartest.'" Get it? You either know or don't know that she's referring to the beauty contest that started the Trojan war and, thus, you will think her remark is either hilarious and wickedly challenging or just a bit odd and maybe a little offensive.

Once I was talking with another student in a corridor lined by faculty offices. Mrs. Preus peeked out of her door and said, "You two have studied Latin. Come read this."

She had taped an article from *Punch* on her door that told a love story about a Roman farmer and his beloved in the style, sentence structure, and limited vocabulary of the old beginning-Latin grammars. The three of us bent our heads together, read silently, giggled in unison, read, giggled, right down the page. It's a tribute to the parodist that we sounded like we had practiced laughing on cue for weeks. But, without that shared background,

Prologue: Tacit Knowledge

both the humor and the presence of that article on a seminary faculty door would be beyond comprehension.

Another time, I was sitting next to Mrs. Preus at a lecture that must have been about the early church because somehow the Visigoths came up.

Mrs. Preus elbowed me and whispered, "The Visigoths weren't the worst of the barbarians."

I smiled, waiting.

She continued, "The Invisigoths were the worst." Now she waited, eyes bright, smile tugging at her mouth, expectant.

I drove in the nail: "Because you couldn't see them."

A quick little nod, an almost silent chuckle, return to the lecture. If you don't find encounters like this hilarious, I probably can't help you.

When you are finally certified for ordination and there is a congregation that has issued you a call to serve as a pastor, then and only then are you ordained. For this ceremony, you also must have someone who is willing to present you as a candidate. I always found this an attractive part of church life, that so often there are occasions when our own voice is not enough and others must speak for us.

Most ordinands choose a pastor: someone they grew up with, a teacher they studied with. For reasons I can no longer recover, though my choice still seems natural and right, I asked Mrs. Preus to be my sponsor. Since I had a reputation as a fairly formal person, with a high view of liturgy and ministry, this might have surprised some people.

But as Mrs. Preus often said, someone who had grown up in a parsonage as she did, especially with a name like Preus, could not really be considered a layperson. (Let me add that Preus was her maiden name. She married another Preus, another pastor.)

Now, if you are a Lutheran of a certain age and background, you will already know what she meant. This is my second example of tacit knowledge. When I entered seminary and started picking up the cues and shorthand of Lutheran church politics, the name of Preus was something like the name of Daley in Chicago or that of Kennedy in Massachusetts: instantly recognizable, conjuring up long service, enduring presence, power both visible and silent, backroom deals, and a kind of royal privilege. The difference would be that there were more of them. It would be as though half the governors and mayors in the United States were all Kennedys, the most distant relation being third cousin.

Prologue: Tacit Knowledge

Now to my point of prologue: I have been speaking of worlds I grew up in and worlds I lived in for years, somewhat closed worlds that can still be made accessible. But these reflections are necessary prologue to all that follows—the memories, stories, fictions of my years as a Lutheran pastor in rural Minnesota. That was a world I see as more closed than my examples, less open to the outsider.

Serving pastors socialize with very few people that aren't pastors or the families of pastors. They may appear to. You may think I'm exaggerating. But they don't really. Every pastor knows: one unguarded word to even your most trusted friend, and an entire community can turn against you. Instantly.

There's an oddness to parsonage life, life in the fishbowl, the glass house. If I say I would much rather do a funeral than a wedding, that I hate Christmas, that I jump when the telephone rings or I hear an ambulance siren, that I end every day in despair at what I have not done, that I am physically ill before church council meetings, or that my kids are helplessly easy targets for criticism and abuse, you may again think I'm exaggerating or being deliberately perverse or just silly. But if you're a pastor, you're nodding your head.

I've sometimes despaired of conveying any real sense of a pastor's life to anyone outside the calling. I suppose one might argue that I would only have written these reflections if I both hoped and expected to be understood. But, after spending over a quarter century as a pastor, I'm not sure any of us know why we do anything.

One more note: I used as one of my epigraphs a famous remark by Hemingway: All remembrance of things past is fiction. I think he meant to note both an inevitability and a deliberate choice. I certainly mean both. Because of what I did and the person I had to be to do what I did, there are things, some of them the most vivid and charged among all the things I recall, that I have never spoken of and never will. If I touch on them, it will be with less than the whole truth. Much less. I expect all the pastors to be nodding again.

Now let me tell you what it was like to be a small town pastor. Really . . .

PART ONE

ALL HANDS STAND BY TO REPEL BOARDERS

THE BEGINNING OF MY service as a pastor was most notable for the mere arrival at the place I was to serve. It had, now that I think of it, something of what missionaries in the nineteenth century must have experienced, setting out from Europe to places that weren't exactly *terra incognita* but were certainly remote, home to strange customs and the human strangeness that grows in isolation, places but sparingly connected to the greater world, places easier to settle in than to return from, places they had never been anywhere near. Also, to further the comparison: in the year I began, cell phones and computers were not nearly as common as they now are. We owned neither.

There's a vivid and indelible memory that comes to me helplessly when I think back to starting out: our little family of four, plus an old beagle who would die in a year, are traveling in two rented trucks, with all our worldly goods, towing our car. It's December 7, 1982, and the temperature is twenty below zero. All our houseplants will freeze and die on this trip. I am in one truck with our daughter; my wife is with our son and the dog in the other. It's about 8:30 at night, we've been driving north from Minneapolis, Minnesota all day, and we've just turned off Interstate 29 in North Dakota, to head east into Minnesota again. We have never seen the town we are heading for, not even in pictures. A Chicago boy, I have never been this far north or west. As I look out the window of the truck, I think I have never seen country so flat, so barren, so sparsely settled. The tiny towns are six miles or more apart. Even the yard lights on the farms are rare, and the farms themselves are mostly dark, because—I will learn— there are few farmers left. I have never seen night so complete or the night sky so clear and filled with stars. We know we will be meeting some Lutherans at journey's end, but that's about all we know.

It came about this way:

I had wanted to do something else with my life, but it hadn't worked out. With a doctorate in philosophy, I had ended up working as a pipefitter.

Through college, five years of grad school, and a year of teaching at Purdue University, all I wanted, and worked for, was to be a philosophy teacher. Having to let that go was bitter and, during that time, it was the Lutheran church we belonged to that gave me something to live by.

I found there that egalitarianism that should be the center of Christian life but often is not, that sense that there are no real distinctions but all are equal before God. At that time, this meant a great deal to me, and I've never forgotten it. My spouse and I became very involved in the church, its educational programs, its music and worship. Making one of those human recalculations of opportunity and desire, I thought I could be at least some of what I wanted to be by working in the church as a pastor.

My spouse and I attended seminary together, and we were both ordained in the old Lutheran Church in America, one of those ephemeral yet sharply defined stages in the long Lutheran story of uniting and dividing. I've told people over the years that she's the real pastor. They always think I'm kidding, but I'm not. She fits more easily and happily into the role and always saw herself as an active church worker. I wanted to do something else, and being a pastor was really not an all-consuming identity for me. This probably saved me a lot of grief over the years. (A friend of mine, another pastor, remarked to me once that "we are all afraid if we stopped being pastors we'd never go to church." I couldn't imagine saying that. The church offered life; being a pastor was just a job.)

But the difficulties of life reappeared, as they will, when we graduated from seminary. We were a clergy couple and, though the LCA had been ordaining women for a decade, no one quite knew what to do with that inevitable consequence: ministers who are not only married, but married to one another.

In those days, you were supposed to enter your service through your home synod, but our bishop claimed to be unable to place a couple with so many advanced degrees and suggested we explore some remote synod that was always looking for personnel: somewhere like the Red River Valley Synod, which ran along the Canadian border in northwest Minnesota and the Dakotas. So we did.

The bishop of that synod, Harold Lohr, had been an infantry officer in World War II, and, after that, a nuclear chemist. Not much on this earth made Harold Lohr feel unable to act. He said he'd place us but it would take time. Be patient.

All Hands Stand By to Repel Boarders

To make life more interesting, the housing and part-time job we had while going to seminary was terminated, and we became nomads. Having graduated in June, we were still looking for work in November, patience getting a little worn.

Finally, one night, the bishop called us after 11:00.

"Got a Minnesota map?"

We did.

"Get it out. Find the Twin Cities. Now go straight up the map until you hit Canada, then turn left and go until you hit North Dakota. Mind going that far north?"

Nope.

"Good. That's where you're going. I'm just sending you, we're not even going to have an interview. When can you get there?"

Our son had broken his elbow the winter before, and we had an appointment with a pediatric orthopedist in Minneapolis on December 7.

"Mind driving all day?"

Nope.

"I'll tell them you'll be there that night—could be late, but you'll be there. They'll be waiting with the keys to the parsonage. Sound good?"

It did.

Even at the time, this would have counted as a fairly unusual arrangement. Pastoral candidates today, filling out pages and pages of self-description and self-evaluation, receiving in turn thick packets of congregational self-studies, able to study websites and take virtual tours of churches, meeting for at least one interview, then usually another with an extensive Q&A, must find this process appallingly primitive, almost criminally negligent, stupefyingly simple, dangerously vulnerable to all the disasters all those elaborate studies are supposed to prevent.

But the parish was having unusual troubles. It had been vacant for fourteen months. The former pastor had had a complete breakdown in the wake of a terrible tragedy in his family. In those days, when there was a vacancy, the parish was served by a vice-pastor, usually the nearest LCA pastor, appointed immediately by the bishop. That pastor would preside at one communion service per month, chair the council meetings, make calls on the seriously ill, perform baptisms, weddings, and funerals. The congregation would have to arrange everything else: the education ministry, other visitation, speakers on the other Sundays. The parish we were being sent to was a two-point parish, two congregations in two towns twelve miles apart. The vice-pastor served a church fifteen miles west of them.

Thus, for fourteen months, that pastor had been doing services at three churches, meeting with three church councils, and—most notably—presiding at funerals in three communities. This county, at that time, had the highest death rate in the state of Minnesota. During those fourteen months, besides the normal cycle of parish deaths, four council members at one of the churches died.

They had interviewed some candidates, but very few people wanted to serve in such an isolated area. They offered the call to a single woman they interviewed, but she turned them down. I think this shocked them a little because they felt they were doing her a favor by calling her. (One council member told me, a few years later, that some of the questions at her interview were pretty abusive. One of them was: "Are we going to see you walking around the lake in a bikini holding a can of beer?" If you probe the assumptions behind that question, you'll understand a lot about rural life at that time.)

The vice-pastor told the bishop he was on the point of having a breakdown himself. So the bishop presented his offer to the parish: he had a clergy couple he wanted to place; he would send them without interview or discussion; they would serve together and be paid as one pastor; after six months, the couple or the parish could terminate the relationship, no questions asked; on the other hand, if both the couple and the parish were willing, the parish would issue a formal call.

They agreed and we were on our way.

Those remote highways in Minnesota can be lonely roads. I remember the relief I felt when we finally reached the town our smaller church was in. We turned north, heading for the smaller town that held—in a nice touch of symmetry—the larger church and the parsonage. I got a jolt when we made the turn and saw a mileage sign: Canada, 30 miles. The sign also listed: Eidsvold, 6 miles. When we went through Eidsvold, I thought I had never seen a town that small that rated a mention on a sign. My next thought was: we're going to a town that didn't make the sign.

It came upon us quickly. Crossing a small river, we were in it, with a lovely new church building on our right. I drove right by it because I knew we were going to an older church and assumed that couldn't be it. But it was: the old building had burned down ten years before: this was its very attractive successor.

All Hands Stand By to Repel Boarders

We circled the block, parked in the church lot, and there they all were, coming out the door: the complete councils of both churches, some of them up well past their bedtimes, waiting to welcome us and get us settled for the night. We had never seen each other before. More strikingly, we had never been in contact during that long day. We came with the faith they would be there. They waited with the faith we would make it. It probably wasn't a bad way to meet.

We were glad to be starting. Having been unemployed, without housing, we were glad to have a job and a home. The parish called us formally after only a couple months. We served there almost sixteen years.

But we left behind everything and everyone we knew. All four of our parents, still alive when we went, died while we served up there and we missed every death. I barely made it to my mother's funeral: I took the first flight out of the Grand Forks airport after it had been closed for an ice storm; the eighty-mile drive to get there was over solid ice. We might see our families once every other year.

And then, after those sixteen years, we left all those things and all those people we knew there, and started up again in another unknown place. By that time, we had grandchildren, but they lived so far away we were lucky to see them once a year.

I think of waking up that first morning, after the long drive across that frozen landscape. We were in sleeping bags, on the floor of the parsonage, and the furnace was roaring. Congregation members would be arriving to unload our trucks.

We got dressed and wandered here and there, exploring the house.

The only people we knew within hundreds of miles were each other. I remember, then, getting one of those lurches of the spirit, when you suddenly want to draw back from something you can really no longer avoid, like freaking out on the high board in a swimming pool. I heard car doors slamming, voices.

From the living room window, I could see people approaching the front door, others walking up the driveway to the side door. More cars were pulling up to the curb. My wife was in the kitchen, I think. The kids were upstairs.

I turned away from the window, cupped my hands around my mouth, and shouted, "All hands stand by to repel boarders!"

I heard my son laugh.

I had always hoped I would find some occasion in life to use that line, and I guess I found it that morning.

I think there was some part of me that meant it, that wanted to go back to something familiar somewhere, that wanted us to repel those friendly, helpful boarders, get back in our rented trucks and get away.

But we were up against that decisive fact in the lives of earthly creatures: we had nowhere else to go.

So we opened the doors, and let them in, and began weaving together the words and deeds that would be our life together, the only life we had.

Caveat Lector

That we would serve as co-pastors in the same parish was not something my wife and I planned or asked for. In fact, the first interviews we had in the Red River Valley Synod were in neighboring parishes. One interview fell through, so Bishop Lohr told us to turn down the other and he would keep trying to place us. Once we had served together for so many years, however, we were unwilling to give up the advantages this gave us; so, when we looked for a new call, we looked together for one. Thus, all the years we served as pastors we served together.

That shared service will not make many explicit appearances in these memories, tales, and reflections. The reader should assume it as background, but I will not be discussing it much. This will, no doubt, make these fragments even more distorted than faulty memory and deliberate alteration have already made them.

Caveat Lector.

However, I thought it might be useful to set down the advantages we found in this arrangement and some of the principles we tried to live and work by. This might also throw some light on my reticence.

The great advantage is time: you get the time to work on your sermon because someone else is doing the visiting that week; you get time to make those visits next week because someone else will be doing that week's sermon. Time, and more than time—it's a rare gift for a serving pastor to hear someone else preach regularly.

Also, if there's a funeral on Friday and a wedding on Saturday with Sunday still to come—and sometimes more—at least you won't be burdened with all of them. (What it's like to find the words for a young person's burial in the morning, then the words for a happy couple's wedding a few hours later, is simply beyond telling.)

We set our week and our tasks by who would prepare Sunday's sermon: that person was in the office that week, studying, preparing the service, dealing with whatever came through the door. The other person did the visiting, the hospital trips, anything that required being on the road. (When the major hospitals are fifty to a hundred miles away, this means a lot.)

Essential things we did together: all worship services (including funerals and weddings, which we understood as congregational milestones), council meetings, major educational events. We alternated Vacation Bible School by the year, confirmation by the half-year, and we split up committees.

But there's one absolute about a team ministry, whether your partner is spouse, friend, stranger, or enemy: if you have to be the center of attention, if you have to shine more brightly than anyone else, if you need to control anything you see as important, if you need the credit, the name above the title, then don't do it. Don't serve in a team ministry, or on a staff. In fact, do me a favor and don't be a pastor. Be a politician or talk show host instead.

Paul's hymn to love, which most of us know from its use at weddings, was meant much more broadly, as a call to life in community: it remains just as vital for the smaller community of the church staff:

Love is patient; love is kind; love is not envious or boastful or arrogant or rude. It does not insist on its own way [repeat this over and over while you're brushing your teeth]; it is not irritable or resentful; it does not rejoice in wrongdoing . . . (1 Cor 13: 4–6)

That's the secret. Piece of cake.

Now I'll note three pieces of advice I acquired over the years that I thought were essential principles for partnership.

1/ Don't split your own congregation. Wherever two leaders are gathered together, there will be a third person trying to play one off against the other. Don't make this easy to do.

I got this advice from an older head pastor who had a long record of good relationships with his assistants. He gave the advice about preaching schedules: he never alternated assignments but staggered them so that no one could come only to hear one person on the staff preach. But obviously the advice goes beyond scheduling.

There are always people willing to tell you how much better you are at something than your partner is. You can't stop this from starting, but you can stop it from continuing. However, if you need to hear this or if you resent that someone else is hearing it, I'll say once more: do not serve in a team ministry. You'll split the congregation apart.

2/ Don't argue in public. There are no perfect choices, approaches, strategies, or styles in church life. No two pastors will agree on all of them. One of you will want to fill the service with music from a website called something like "New hymns with impossible rhythms that no one on earth has ever heard"; the other won't be able to understand what's wrong with singing some version of "Old One Hundredth" every week. Settle it in the office. Settle it and let it go. Don't debate it at the council meeting. Don't evaluate it in the narthex with your fans after the service. Speak with one voice.

It might seem more honest, more ingenuous, more open, to debate these things freely with everyone, to let people know you disagree. In one sense, that's true. I didn't mind people knowing we disagreed and compromised, but it was more important that they knew we finally agreed and supported the same decision. Also, knowing we disagreed was one thing, seeing it fought out was another. Any open, extreme disagreement will inevitably be exploited by someone else for their own purposes. You can't let that happen.

3/ Respect each other's work. Don't look over each other's shoulders. If one of you is writing the sermon, leading the adult class, planning the funeral or the wedding, negotiating with the budget committee, prioritizing visitation, let that be that. Certainly, a staff should talk, share ideas, settle on strategies and directions, evaluate what worked and what didn't. But there's a point where you have to accept the fact that the call to ministry and the authority of word and sacrament are no greater for you than for your partner.

Also, it never hurts to speak some words of praise.

Now, somewhere in the above reflections, you should be able to find a reason why our shared ministry is the background, not the subject, of this writing of mine.

Extremely Isolated, Extremely Cold, Extremely Dark

Our first morning in our first call was very still, very bright, very cold. It was twenty below zero, and it had been that cold for days. The ground was like steel: walking, you expected it to clang. The air was thin, sharp: breathing, you thought your lungs might crack.

From the parsonage yard, you could see both the north and the south edge of town. Beyond them, all you saw were flat, empty fields, extending farther than you would want to walk in a day. A joke I would hear every year for the next couple of decades went like this: "Well, this isn't the end of the world. But you can just about see it from here." While the congregation helped us unload our trucks, my daughter announced she was going to walk downtown and see what it had to offer.

About an hour later, I saw she had returned. She was sitting on a chair in the kitchen, out of the way, slumped down, staring at nothing. I walked over, she moved her eyes slightly to acknowledge my presence.

I said, "And the verdict is—?"

"I'm going to go upstairs and hang myself." She stood up and left the room. It was a great exit line.

(I will note, to reassure the reader, that she did not, in fact, hang herself. Her more considered judgment, delivered that night, was that she would finish school, move to a city, and never return. And that's what she did, living her adult life in New York and Chicago. Her idea of a vacation is to go to London, Paris, or Los Angeles. Her idea of a visit to the wilderness is to go to Atlanta or Milwaukee.)

People were always telling me "this is a great place to raise kids," but I was never sure even they believed it. They would usually say it as though that was the consolation prize for living in a place so remote, with so little to offer. It was a fifty-mile drive to a decent movie theatre; if you wanted a choice of movies, it was an eighty-mile drive. The same was true of anything else you might want that was a cut above the basic, from clothing to groceries to sports gear to wine.

I think, at best, that remark about raising children had more to do with the fear of parents than with any benefit to youth. They felt they didn't have to worry as much as they might in a bigger town. At worst, the remark was a coded rejection of the racial and ethnic diversity they might have to face elsewhere. I met people who were still outraged that Martin Luther King's birthday was a holiday. But growing up with people exactly like you, half of whom you're related to, whose major life goals are getting a driver's license and killing their first deer, seems to me no advantage at all to a young person, let alone a great one.

The teachers I knew made heroic efforts to bring as much of the world as they could to their students. But as the rural areas lost population, the schools were collapsing into themselves: consolidating, cutting budgets, offering less. The same was true of every other institution that might sustain a community, from hospitals to hardware stores to police departments to churches.

There were barely three hundred people in our town, only five thousand in the entire county. Our town had no doctor, no dentist, no police officer. The nearest hospital was twelve miles away when we came; after it closed, the nearest was fifteen, with a doctor so dismissive of people's complaints he was known as "Doctor Death." The sheriff's office, which had to do more and more of the law enforcement, was fifteen miles away.

One year, on Halloween, all the street lights were shot out. Another year, somebody shot up the bank: the bank tellers had their picture taken for the local paper pointing to the hole in the wall, as they might have done when Wyatt Earp was still alive. (By the time we left, the bank was gone, too.)

But the thing that really isolated you was the winter, especially the extreme cold.

I was up one January night, unable to sleep. We had an old mercury thermometer just outside the kitchen window. (Because of the heat loss through the window, the thermometer would usually register a little higher than the actual temperature.) To torture myself mentally, I tried to see how cold it was, but I couldn't make out the mercury in the tube. I got a flashlight and shined it through the window. There was no mercury: it had dropped below the forty below line and was huddled in the bottom of the tube, like a wounded animal.

It could be forty below zero for weeks. People made a valiant attempt to keep their lives going but it took a real effort to leave the house for anything but the most necessary trips and, by the end of January, the isolation would be getting to everybody.

We did a funeral one spring after a horrible cold spell. During the funeral lunch, we were talking to some of the relatives who had come quite a distance. The conversation, as it often does in Minnesota, turned to winter weather. One of the out-of-town ladies shrugged and said, "Well, cold is cold. So you just dress up. What's the big deal?"

The locals stared at her in disbelief. One said, "You don't go outside much, do you?" Another said, "And you sure aren't from around here."

It's hard to convey how devastating extreme cold can be to someone who's never experienced it. Once you're used to northern Minnesota, ten below is fairly tolerable with a good parka, but twenty below makes your parka feel like a windbreaker. At forty below, that same parka will feel like a light shirt, and you had better respect how deadly the temperature has become. People that knew more than I knew, or wanted to know, said there was a corresponding impact at sixty below.

All the cars had engine-block heaters, and we plugged them in if we wanted the motor to turn over in the morning. We never left the driveway without sleeping bags and a survival kit in the trunk. In the worst cold, you had to put a cover over your radiator grille so your engine wouldn't freeze. The car heater could barely keep the frost off the inside windows.

I remember the sensation of going in and out: having that first cold breath scorch your lungs and feeling the chill come right through your clothes; then, after being numbed and pushed inside yourself outside, having the heat blast over you when you entered a building, getting groggy from the warmth.

I remember lingering in gas stations, enjoying that instant camaraderie of all the poor souls that had to be on the road, laughing at how bad it was, asking about road conditions.

Because it wasn't just the cold that hung on: the snow might cover the ground for six months, from the beginning of October to the end of March. Of course, before and after those dates, there might be snowfalls and ice storms that would linger for a few days.

Late one evening, I was coming back from a hospital visit. I stopped for gas and ran into one of the men who worked for the town, plowing the streets, mowing city property, doing general maintenance. He had moved

Extremely Isolated, Extremely Cold, Extremely Dark

to the area to manage the hardware store before it went out of business and ended up being stranded. It had been an unusually bad year for snow, even by our standards, and we were, a bit hysterically, joking about how bad it might get and where we would put the snow if it was still coming in June.

"Don't laugh," he said. "I've seen it snow in June. In fact, one year we had such miserable weather, I was standing right here—right here pumping gas—on the Fourth of July. We'd been out watching the fireworks. I looked up and there was snow coming down. Not much, melted right away, but there they were: snowflakes on the Fourth of July. So I've seen snow in this country every damned month of the year."

But you could laugh about that; it was the deep winter that was frightening. Driving home late, ice on the roads, snow falling through your headlights, no other cars in sight, miles between one town and the next, and—in the early years—no cell phones, no car navigation systems, none of the connections we cling to now, you appreciated what a tiny, vulnerable organism you were, how much your small spark of life was up against.

And above you, in that clear, frigid air, was the dark beauty of the universe, with hardly any ground lights to blind you to it. Before those nights in Minnesota, I had never seen so many stars so clearly. Especially after a long drive, or after a long walk in the summer, your night vision would get better and you could see the clusters and clumps of the galaxies as you never can in the city. And it was one of the better places on earth to see the light shows of the northern lights. I had read about them but, seeing them through the windshield for the first time, I couldn't believe what I was looking at.

That was where I learned to identify the constellations. I got the book on the stars written by H. A. Rey, who wrote the Curious George books our kids loved, and I had a great time running in and out, trying to match diagrams to reality.

At our bigger church, which we lived next to, there was a path on the west side, going from the parsonage to the parking lot and the main entrance. I tried to keep it clear in the winter, and one of my indelible memories is walking to night meetings between piles of snow four feet high, looking right at the North Star, and, coming home a couple of hours later, looking up at Orion.

But, obviously, it was easier to stay out and stare up at the sky in the summer. I felt triumphant one night when I could finally pick out Hercules and the Serpent Holder. I would lie on our front lawn, with its gentle slope down to the highway, and lose myself in the vast beauty of those long-travelling beams of light that still look like points on a dome. The universe became my friend. A cold and distant friend, but a peaceful and undemanding one, ever present, ever welcoming. Lying on my back, looking up happily, losing myself, I could feel the deep kinship of matter that we've taught ourselves: the stars, the earth and my breathing flesh all made of the same stuff.

On my worst days, those would be good moments.

Beating the Bounds

I had, at seminary, an eccentric church history professor who never came to class without his copy of the *Oxford Dictionary of the Christian Church*. He loved finding a pretext to consult this thick tome—some obscure ceremony or odd breakaway sect—and would read the entire entry aloud, giggling delightedly. He thought all pastors of the church should have a copy on their desks, so I bought one. It's still sitting in front of me, still regularly consulted.

One Saturday, I was looking for an odd detail to spice up my sermon and, for some reason I can no longer remember, looked up the article on "Beards, Clerical."

A bound reference work, like the physical stacks of a library, offers a pleasure not to be had from those pinpoint internet searches: stumbling across an utterly unrelated, but fascinating, entry. In the column across from "Beards, Clerical," I saw an entry titled "Beating the Bounds," so I read that instead.

Beating the bounds was an old early summer ceremony in medieval England, when prayers would be offered for the harvest. The annual procession would trace the boundaries of the parish, beating them with willow rods or—and this is the fun part—bumping the boys of the parish on the ground at the boundary. (The article says the boys were "also beaten." Intriguingly, it ends by noting a modern—I have the 1978 edition—revival. I thought this was a typical religious blend of reasonable purpose and thinly disguised sadism, so familiar to me from my Roman Catholic youth.)

In our time and place, religious division and variety make the idea of firm parish boundaries impossible. The automobile has also done its part in scrambling them. Driving from one of the small churches we served to the other on Sunday morning, we would pass several other churches and many other drivers traveling past our churches to reach theirs.

Still, in a small town, it's easy to think of that town as the rough, if porous, boundary of the parish. I reflected, after reading that article, that in any given week I did my own version of the ceremony.

Looking back on my service, I consider this one of the greatest pieces of luck I had: that I could do so much of what I had to do on foot, some of it on dirt roads leading to the grassy paths of small cottages hidden by trees. On quiet days, I could imagine I might bump into Thomas Hardy or Anthony Trollope. I had acquired, over the years, a collection of stout, gnarled walking sticks, which helped complete my fantasy.

I couldn't exactly circumnavigate the towns we lived in, because they were bounded by rivers, planted fields, thick woods, and barbed wire. But, in both of them, I could walk out to the edge and back in every direction, all in an easy half-day.

Our first town was smaller and dropped off quickly into farms. The land was flat there and a lot of my walking was on gravel roads. Our second town was in a deep valley and you had to go up a fairly steep grade whichever side you walked out. It was also more built-up and had sidewalks as well as paved roads. To both the east and west, there were cemeteries. (In our first parish, the cemetery was across the street from the parsonage. It was the first thing I saw when I looked out the window in the morning.)

I would typically do my visiting in the afternoons. I loved walking along with my home communion kit and my Occasional Services book in my shoulder bag, whistling and twirling my walking stick. People would always ask me where I left my car. But once an old fellow I met said, "Doing your parish rounds, eh?" and I was ridiculously pleased to be able to say, "I am."

But my most frequent walk was in the morning, to the post office to get the mail. There was a rural mail carrier for the farms, but most people in town rented a box. This was a great meeting place, somewhere to hear the news and take the measure of current opinion, find out why the sirens went off last night, and finally bump into someone you'd been trying to contact for days. Depending on the character of the postmaster, she (or, less often, he) could be very much the ringmaster of this arena, having final judgment on matters of fact and practicality. Depending, again, on the postmaster, I could sometimes spend an hour at the desk, catching up on current events or filling in the history of local feuds.

I tended not to vary my path, and I couldn't have varied it much. So my walk there was almost an extension of my office hours: people knew when I'd be passing by, and it was a good way to contact me if you didn't want people to wonder what you were doing at the church. It wasn't odd for me to spend an hour on the half-mile walk.

I would pass the jumbled life of the old small towns: houses, welding shops that still rang with the blacksmith's hammer, a grocery store, a body shop, a gas station. I could just glimpse the closest farms and watch the plowing or harvesting. In our second parish, if I walked far enough out of town, I could see the plowing being done with horses, since we had a growing Amish community around us.

My walk in our second parish took me past a small branch of the regional library system, housed in an old building with the town museum. (Where we first served, the nearest library was fifteen miles away, the nearest decent library was fifty miles away, and the bookmobile stopped every three weeks for about forty-five minutes.) I could continue up the hill out of town and drop in on the staff at the high school.

The big difference in my walks was that, in our first parish, the parsonage was next to the church, so my walk was to the post office and back, while, in our second parish, the parsonage was a half-mile from the church, so I continued on after my post-office visit to the church office. I had stops along the way in each town, about mid-journey, very important for my survival when the temperature was below zero and the wind was howling, always important for my spirit because I found the most pleasant people there and they always lifted my heart.

In our first parish, it was the gas station, run for a minimal profit by a couple named Danny and Patty. Stopping one day, I heard classical music on the radio behind the counter and I knew I'd found some friends. Danny could laugh and Patty could fume at almost anything. Knowing them was like watching a great comedy team. But they were both lively, funny, interested in music, books, and movies, and—I hope—as pleased as I was to find someone else who was.

When I lingered there, I would often bump into one of our substitute organists, Judy, the daughter of one of the matriarchs of the town (whom I thought of as the Queen of Hearts). Judy was a survivor of one of the more radical versions of the 'sixties and would drift into town and out of town on no one's wavelength but her own. My service there overlapped with one of her longer stays. She was an excellent keyboard player and, oddly enough, loved the most elaborate liturgies we used, because they reminded her of Native American ceremonies she'd seen. She dabbled in natural medicine and was always trying to cure me of problems that usually sounded more like hers than mine. She had a deep, explosive, sexy laugh and, sometimes, I'd walk her home and we'd share stories about our youth. It was, I thought, like a dialogue between Passion and Sanity. Once I impressed her by adjusting the idle on her VW bus.

In our second parish, it was the bank, staffed by a group of women I thought of collectively as the Bank Babes. One of them, Mel, was a member of the church we served and the other two, Ginny and Faith, were members of the Methodist church just across the street with which we shared Lenten services. Not only were these women unfailingly pleasant, happily talkative, and very pretty, but all three were also dog- owners and -lovers. As our children were gone by this time, we often needed people to tend to our dog when we were at all-day meetings, two-day church conventions, or late events in the Twin Cities. This was another piece of good luck: finding people I could trust absolutely, without hesitation.

I was happy to leave our second parish: they made it easy to go. But I almost broke down, the day we left, when I went to say goodbye to the Bank Babes.

There were many people I encountered on these walks, regularly, through the years: the jolly woman who owned the grocery store, who would trade mystery novel recommendations with me; the ex-merchant marine seaman, who still swayed as he walked and ran a kind of men's coffee hour that got out just about when I hit the post-office corner; the mercurial Roman Catholic woman who asked me to help her design a tattoo of the Holy Trinity to put on her left breast; my friend Rick, often congregational president, always a wise leader in church and community, who taught history in high school and could burn an hour or more with me dissecting the political scene.

It was always a good way to start the day.

About a year after we retired, we served as interim pastors in a new church built out in the country. We had to drive everywhere. There was nowhere to walk, no one to meet casually. During the week, I'd stare out the window at the empty parking lot. It made me feel completely immobilized.

The Little Trailer on the Corner

Because of the way our first parsonage was sited, we couldn't see a lot of other houses and, happily, not many people could stare very long at ours, unless they were standing in the middle of the highway. We had the church on one side of us and, on the other side, the river that bounded the town on the south. But from our back windows you could look through our yard, full of two dozen oak trees, our own woods, through the next yard, and get a pretty good look at one dwelling, a beat-up trailer that stood on the next corner.

It was right where I made my turn on my walk to the post office every morning. But I wasn't really inside it much until the lady living in it began to fall ill and unravel.

Bernice was a quiet, kind person, a faithful church member, mother of one of our council members, and grandmother of some of our confirmation students. She was small and thin, with graceful movements. I remember her usually smiling and looking happy. She was also clearly of African-American heritage, a rare thing in our remote area, where almost everyone was named some version of Lena Johnson or Magnus Olafson. But it was precisely that Swedish presence that held the key: someone told me two of the early farmers, immigrant brothers, free of the American sickness of racism, had married African-American girls. Bernice was one of their children who had remained in the area, though not the only one.

I knew Bernice as pastors know all the little, white-haired, older ladies in their congregations: as part of the regular crowd—not as well as the more active volunteers, much better than the occasional churchgoers. Since I knew her son and grandchildren, I knew her a little better than most, though not much.

Then one day at church she came over and thanked me for standing outside her trailer and singing to her. I had no idea what she was talking about and, when I pressed her, she gave a nervous laugh and looked away, as though she suspected herself that she was being swallowed by confusion, but insisted that she had heard my wife and me singing in our yard and then coming over to her trailer to serenade her. She assured me it was quite nice.

Well, the church had some chimes that played in the evening, there were a lot of shadows from the trees in those yards, lots of kids out and about, so I thought it was just possible some combination of those circumstances had led her to think what she thought.

But she kept hearing the singing and no one quite knew what to think about it. In a small town where there are so many family connections, people become aware of problems among the elderly fairly quickly. Among regular churchgoers, people are always noticed and quickly missed. Everybody liked Bernice so the puzzle she was presenting got a lot of attention. We started dropping in on her, the family started making doctor appointments, but she still seemed to get around well and function well. She just kept hearing the singing around her trailer.

Then the singing stopped and the abuse began: voices shouting at her, ridiculing her, calling her names. You can imagine the names. I'm sure everything she heard from the white Americans she grew up with, everything she swallowed and smiled her way through, was breaking out of her memory and rioting in her mind. I was horrified to think she might still be imagining my voice among them.

At last, what she heard was no longer an occasional serenade or rant but a constant, relentless, vile commentary on everything she said and did, every movement, every thought.

She said to me once, "Hear it? Why is it saying 'Bernice is rocking, Bernice is talking, Bernice is . . . '" It drove all sense away from her, she really couldn't live alone anymore, and she was put into a nursing home.

Bernice still looked happy when I walked into her room. We might converse a little, then her smile would go a little odd, her eyes search above her, and she would ask me if I could tell where the voices were coming from. She wouldn't repeat everything they said, sometimes just ask "Why would they say those things about me?"

It's hard to sit there when you've known the person in better days. It's hard to leave them when you have to go, and you have some idea of the world they're in.

Finally, I was no longer sure, when I visited, that Bernice knew who I was. There are people who call that a mercy, but I've never been able to. Those lost to our world aren't senseless: they just don't sense us, the order of the human world that's trying to reach them and care for them. They're sensing something else and, unless you're certain it's not horrible, don't talk about mercy. In this case, I'm pretty sure it was horrible.

You could say the real mercy was when she died. I can just about make myself do that, though I can say it more easily about physical suffering than about the suffering of the spirit. But the hard truth is, it really doesn't matter what we say. We're just trying to make ourselves stop thinking, come up with an excuse to make ourselves feel better, get rid of the gnawing memories. It makes no difference to the suffering.

Most of the time, we do stop thinking, feel better, get rid of the worst of the memories, or at least their sting. I still took the same walk to the post office each morning, still turned by her trailer, still thought about her, but less wrenchingly as the weeks and months went by.

If you live long enough in the same place, you start to see its layers: new things coming along, old things gone. You see the physical strands of its life in space and time: this person, that business, this house, that empty lot, in all their relative permanence and impermanence. In rural Minnesota, when I served, it was the impermanence that came most strongly to you. And something more than impermanence: when this town and the farms around it were first built, they were built in hope, to make a life, a future; now—for those still here—it was a matter of hanging on, hanging on here because there was nowhere else to go.

Older people would tell me they used to walk down the street and be able to name all the people they saw, tell you who their parents were, and probably what they had for lunch. Since I was a child of Chicago, this wasn't something I could ever do or ever want to do. But it was a way the people here had wanted to live, a way they treasured, that made them feel at home on the earth, and it was gone.

Bernice's trailer stayed empty for a time, then some young people I didn't really know moved in. There were a number of young people drifting around the area, renting rundown trailers, houses, rooms over empty stores. Leaving high school might be the last significant event in their lives. They were usually, if distantly, related to one or more of the older families, but they kept away from regular contacts with the community. You'd see them for a while, then you wouldn't, and they'd be in some other trailer in some other town. You'd glimpse a couple and a child, then only the woman and child, then no one.

As I recall, I was vaguely aware someone was occupying the trailer, vaguely aware there might be a small child, but I can't say I ever saw them in the yard or ran into them on the street or glimpsed any sign of living going on, happy or not.

Then one night I woke out of wild, violent dreams. Our bedroom was at the back of the house and I saw light filling the room, rippling on the walls, blazing through the curtains. I looked out and saw a great, living fire across the yard, with the trailer dark inside it.

I told my wife to dial emergency, grabbed some clothes and ran outside, round the church to the trailer. If I had any thought of getting someone out, the fire crushed it immediately. The heat was so powerful I couldn't step from the street to the yard. It was like hitting a wall that started to turn your skin into something else and pull it off you. I looked around and thought at most I could offer shelter if anyone had managed to get out. I stared at the fire, the way you always stare at fires, only this one was rising far above my head and many times my size, and my stomach turned with the sure and certain knowledge that it was as impossible to leave that fire as it was to enter it.

The fire siren was wailing. I thought maybe I'd hang around until the fire department arrived, just in case anyone did stumble out of the darkness.

Then someone did. She came strolling up the street as though she were taking an afternoon walk. Standing next to the fire in the middle of the night, I could see very little else, so she gave me a start when she materialized.

She was another of our church members, a strange woman, daughter of one of the men who did odd jobs in town, who still lived with him. I'd heard some rumors of her past but you hear lots of things as a small-town pastor, not always told with the best of motives or much concern with accuracy. She showed up at church services and events, and she struck me as just one more town character, maybe a little harsher than most.

She walked up to me, looking from side to side, not meeting my eyes, nodded in my direction, then stood next to me, her arms folded.

I was about to ask her if she knew if anyone had been in the trailer when she said: "I hope they burn to a crisp."

Then she nodded at the fire, turned back the way she had come, and disappeared in the dark.

It was like being next to another, greater, more overwhelming fire, but a fire of another order than physical. I've thought of something like napalm, that sticks to your spirit and you can't get it off. I truly can't remember anything else that happened that night: the fire trucks arriving, talking to the volunteers, walking home, telling my wife what happened. The encounter with the woman has darkened everything else for me.

I found out the next day that no one had been inside the trailer during the fire. Whoever had been living there had moved on to another run-down dwelling in another town.

It's that handful of words spoken by my strange night companion that stays with me. I've tried over the years to describe to myself what it was like, at that moment, to hear something like that: an image that comes to me is something like a trapdoor thudding open right at my feet, showing some dark well of human horror.

But all the comparisons seem weak. Nothing I say now that I felt or thought can capture what confronted me. I finally decided that's because I really didn't think or feel anything. When I probe that memory, it's like I've gone numb, the way your body can go numb immediately at the point of an injury.

It's the image of her, her words, the ugly passion, that stays before me. I can see her right now more vividly than I can see most of my life and service: the quick, affirming nod at the fire, turning away from me, walking out of the light, leaving me staring after her, alone.

What's a Nice Philosopher like You Doing in a Profession like This?

When I first studied philosophy, my teacher was a Methodist minister with a passionate commitment to phenomenology and existentialism. Like so many twentieth-century thinkers (not only the existentialists), he gave the impression philosophy only began getting answers in modern times. The negative side of this teaching, of course, was that I had a lot of catching up to do, as well as prejudices to overcome, when I began seriously studying philosophy's history. (I found it very profitable to read, when I was a serving pastor, Spinoza's *Ethics*, which I would have scorned to open as an undergraduate.)

But the positive side of beginning philosophy with a Christian existentialist was that it cast the whole endeavor of philosophy as a way of living, not merely of learning (or, worse yet, unraveling logical puzzles). Not being able to teach philosophy, as I had hoped to do, didn't mean I lost the point of studying it. You could say the point was sharpened.

In any case, this probably eased my way into working for the church and helped give my life a continuity it might not have had.

· My way was eased, from the other side, by my admiration for Christians like Dietrich Bonhoeffer, Thomas Merton, and Daniel Berrigan. At the time, I probably couldn't have worked for the church if I didn't think people like that were at the heart of the church. I thought they were leading lives I would have called philosophical (much more so than the academics who called themselves philosophers). These were lives that loved wisdom, sought wisdom, lives that tried to think, act, and feel wisely, lives that paid a price, as Socrates did, for their choices, their activities.

As Socrates did, as Jesus did. Towards the end of my service, I used to say, partly to be provocative but mostly to be honest, that I wasn't a Christian because I believed God created the world (or that humans had souls or that there was a heaven waiting for good little boys and girls): I was a Christian because I couldn't get away from Jesus, from the stories he told to snare us in his world, from the stories told of his time in our world.

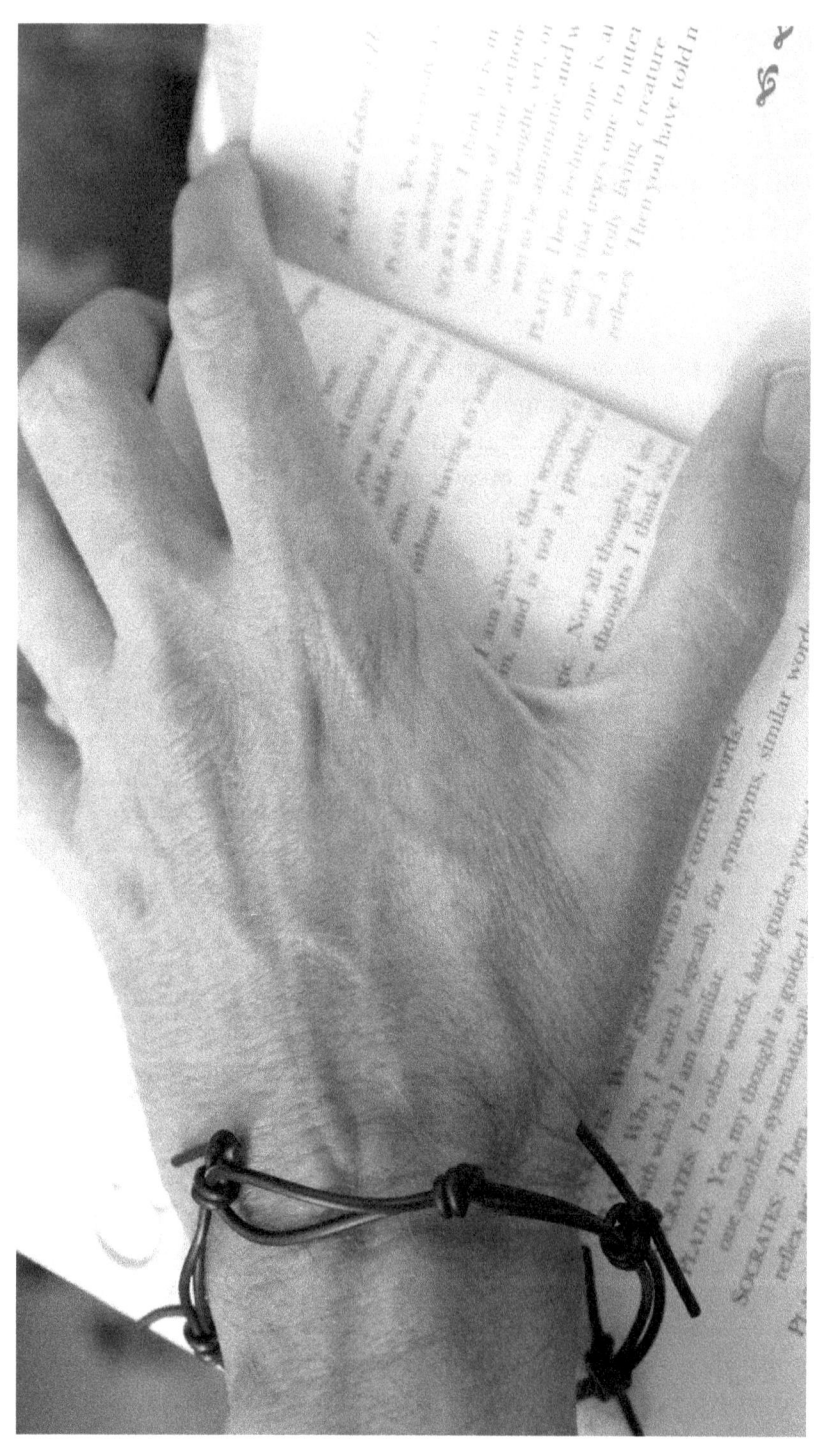

What's a Nice Philosopher like You Doing in a Profession like This?

    I don't think Jesus and Socrates would have had a hard time recognizing each other, or Jesus and Diogenes the Cynic, for that matter. (In fact, John the Baptist, Jesus, and Paul don't make a bad philosophical trio.) The simple life pictured in the gospels, the scorn of the world's pomp and glitter, the self-possessed courage before earthly power, the sense that grew among the Christians that they were citizens not of a tribe but of the world, are elements in a life that most of the children of Socrates would find congenial. Paul's boast in Philippians could have been spoken by many of them:

    I have learned to be content with whatever I have. I know what it is to have little, and I know what it is to have plenty. In any and all circumstances I have learned the secret of being well-fed and of going hungry, of having plenty and of being in need. (Phil 4: 11–12)

    Given this convergence, I came to think, as I grew older, that the path of wise living wasn't really that hard to find. It was, as always, living it, wanting it in the first place, that was the problem.

Holy Things

THERE WAS A LITTLE café on the south side of town in our first parish. It was just across the river from the parsonage yard, an easy walk down the highway. We'd eat there sometimes if we were hosting a pastors' meeting and, at first, we thought it would be a handy place to grab a quick lunch or to treat ourselves to dinner. This turned out to be harder than I thought, especially if we wanted to eat our food quickly, or taste it while it was still warm.

Everyone in town who was on the church's books but who would never enter the church except for weddings and funerals would stroll over to our table, greet us not as distant acquaintances but as bosom companions, and stand there hovering until whatever we ordered had begun to decompose. They'd tell stories, share philosophical reflections, and generally make me perspire with impatience and discomfort. Then they would sigh in satisfaction and depart, proclaiming some variation of: "Well, I'd better let you eat your dinner." They would sometimes add: " . . . so you can get back to work."

In a way, it was another version of church membership: they really did want us to know them and to know they considered themselves members. (They wanted everybody to know it. That's why they hovered so long.) And, to be honest, they weren't the worst members the church had. They just made eating in town impossible. If we were going to dine out, we had to leave town and, eventually, as more people knew us, leave the county. (Or order something that could be eaten cold.)

One of the people I met this way was a tall, thin, rugged-looking old fellow, with a stately walk and a quiet manner, named Arlan. I knew a lot of his kids and grandkids since the family really was strongly connected to the church; his wife was a mainstay of the women's group, especially if cooking was needed.

Arlan not only looked like he'd stepped out of the nineteenth-century frontier, he tried to live as though he were still there. He and his wife had a little farm, and they still cooked on a wood-burning stove. She baked all their bread in this contraption. It pained Arlan to buy anything he could make himself—or have his wife make.

There was an obsessive minimalism to him. He liked getting by with little and worked at getting by with less and less. I offered him a cup of coffee once and he scoffed at the idea, proudly declaring he drank nothing but water. (I helplessly thought of General Ripper from *Dr. Strangelove*.)

I liked Arlan and, despite his quirks, had a lot of respect for him. He was bull-headed and he didn't have the broadest outlook on life, but he had a commanding air, great natural dignity. He drove one of the school buses, and I heard his discipline was both absolute and effortless.

One day, after one of the milestones of life—birth, marriage, or death—had brought Arlan to the church grounds, we were talking on the front lawn, beneath the large cross on the church's brick front. Arlan pointed at the church's name, very elegantly set in metal letters across the brick. He said, "I gave those letters in memory of my daughter. She died in a car wreck the year they rebuilt after the fire." It was characteristic of Arlan that he gave me no other information, just noted the memorial and the reason. But it was a proud and solemn pronouncement, and it was a moment with something to say about church and community.

For this man who never came to a regular worship service, this place was holy ground, a fitting site for holy things, things set apart in devotion and love.

(A few years later, Arlan's wife, Flo, was killed in a freak road accident when they were on one of the few vacations they ever took. I told someone that doing that funeral was like burying my grandmother. After the funeral, Arlan gave us a dozen rolls Flo had baked and frozen before the trip. She was a fabulous baker, but I had a hard time bringing myself to eat them: it was like eating consecrated bread.)

I used to point out to my confirmation students that there's no scene in the New Testament that depicts Jesus telling his disciples to write down what's going on. I was trying to make them think about the essentials of faith and the growth of tradition. Jesus never tells his disciples to get busy and build churches either. Yet Bibles and buildings are part of the reality of Christian faith. It's not only impossible, by now, to think of Christianity without its writings and places of worship; it's impossible to think of this community enduring through time without preserving its stories or venerating the sites of its central acts.

Births and deaths happen where they happen, but a community brings the babies and those prepared for burial to the place of worship for those events to be marked, marked by symbols of a greater life. It's the action of marking that gives weight to the site. Baptize enough babies, marry enough men and women, say the last words over enough loved ones in the same place and you can't think of it as anything but holy ground.

But that place is there for those times only because it's there already for something more encompassing: it's the place we enact the primary rituals of faith, every week of every year for as long as the community lives.

This is the dominating rhythm of every pastor's life. Everything I did, everything that happened to me, all the things I'm setting down in these fragments, happened within the movement of each week toward the Sunday service, and the place of that Sunday in the cycle of the church year. Both the joys and the sorrows were tempered by the worship cycle. (One more thing for the reader to remember.)

It's not hard for most people to appreciate the beauty of ritual, but I think its power, its force over a community, the way it steadies and broadens life, can only be grasped if you're living with its rhythms. In a strange way, the stylized world of ritual and symbol takes you out of your life and into a greater life. That's where the steadiness comes from.

There are always reformers around who want to dissolve "Sunday" into "Monday" concerns, as though faith would be enriched that way. It never seems to occur to them that faith could just as easily be impoverished by the pettiness and provincialism most people's ordinary lives are overwhelmed by. I often thought, when we prayed the Prayer of the Church, that many of us were being forced to think and feel beyond our own lives in a way we seldom did otherwise. I thought, in any given week, the Sunday gathering was probably the most profound encounter most of us had with thought, music, history, and the great world beyond our little place.

(On a smaller scale, I was always amazed how quickly and surely the Lord's Prayer could steady and uphold a roomful of grieving mourners.)

I saw once a stole worn by one of the pastors who was trying to make the traditional Sunday more reflective of ordinary life: instead of the symbols of the faith, he had placed on it corporate logos, reflective of the businesses people in his congregation worked for. He looked like a walking billboard.

My first thought was: has this moron ever worked a day in his life for one of these companies? And does he actually imagine people that work for them want to *pray* to them?

My non-attending member Arlan understood more about the presence of the church in a place than this thoughtless clown who served as a pastor.

Hanging Out

You have to love the basic rhythm of church life, the inexorable, unstoppable turning of every week toward Sunday, when, ready or not, you have to bring what you have for everybody to receive. I went into every Sunday energized, stomach turning over, anxious to start, riding that performer's wave of aspiration. I was jittery with nerves until I could enter the service and have it carry me along. Every Sunday was like opening night: it could make you so sick it would be easy to hate it if you didn't love it.

But all around that great moment and that basic rhythm were the sloppier rhythms of ordinary life in a small town parish: the people you see every day in town, the shut-ins you visit, the classes and the meetings, the people going in and out of medical care, the people in nursing homes who are never coming out. The years pass and you bury, baptize, teach, and marry generation after generation in the same families. You have to love that, too.

In grad school, we were members of a university church and the turnover of members was constant. The handful of funerals that occurred during our years there were shattering experiences for that gathering of the young and vibrant. But, during our service as pastors, funerals were a defining mark of the communities we served in, a clearly visible, ever present stage on life's way. When we buried the old ones, children would be taken down the hall of confirmation pictures to see their grandfathers and grandmothers in their confirmation robes.

One long winter, I was reading Siegfried Sassoon's fictionalized memoirs of his service as an infantry officer in World War I, and it struck me that life in a small town parish had some similarities: nobody's winning anything; nobody's going anywhere—in fact, you feel guilty when you leave; all you can do is keep the life you have going with as much courage and humor as you can summon up; when there's a change, it's usually brought by death.

(During one of the worst winters, I started to see myself as something like a junior officer in the doomed German sixth army at Stalingrad: in a trap like that, it made no difference what you knew or what you did; you

Hanging Out

had simply come to a time and place where you were going to lose. I can remember coming up with that comparison as I trudged to the post office in a howling blizzard, but I'm thankfully distant from the depression that must have spawned it.)

And yet I generally enjoyed that weekly, yearly round within the lifetimes of the people who happened to be living at the time and in the place where I happened to be serving.

I had my own personal rhythms my life moved to, as well. It's amusing to look back and realize that in such a public, exposed life, I tended to begin and end each week in absolute solitude. Since every week moved to the Sunday service, I worked hard to keep Saturday night clear. I wanted to get into a tunnel where all I could see were the details of the things to be done next day. (This became such a habit that I still get nervous leaving the house on Saturday night.) The more commitments I had on Sunday the more isolated I wanted to be the night before.

Then, the more things I had done on Sunday the more catatonic I was on Monday morning. I would sit over my coffee, trying to remember what it felt like to be interested in anything.

But it's the regular, gentle drifting along with the lives of others that I want to celebrate here and that I think is so important in parish life.

I was standing, one day, with a pair of young funeral directors, John and Joe. They were the last two in a series of fine funeral directors I was thankful to work with. The three of us would often be, except for a couple of ladies in the kitchen, the first to arrive at a funeral. I needed to check everything not only well before the service but well before any mourners arrived. I had nothing but contempt for leaders who weren't prepared and it was a pleasure to work with people who thought the same.

John and Joe always treated the presiding ministers to lunch after we were set up. Then we would stroll back to the church to deal with anything that came up; but, mostly, if things were going smoothly, we would talk to the mourners and hang out together.

I was standing there with them, enjoying the comfortable way we worked together, feeling good about all the people that had turned out for the service, seeing such a big part of the community flowing together for this moment, and that was when I had this reflection: if someone asked me what you needed, if you were going to thrive as a pastor, I think I would say that, after you reach a certain level of competence with the standard qualifications, there's one quality you have to have. You have to be able, sometimes, to do nothing much but hang out.

Saint Ken

Once we were settled into our first parish, Pastor Walt, the pastor who had served so many months as vice-pastor when the parish was vacant, dropped in to see how we were doing and to give us whatever information he thought we needed immediately. Before he left, he talked a little about the pastors in the conference. Since the area was so isolated, they tended to make a point of getting together regularly. He urged us to show up at the meetings. He said we'd find them a good group, and we did. Then he said, "You'll be meeting Ken soon."

Ken was the pastor of the largest LCA church in the county, north of Walt and west of us. Walt smiled and continued, "He won't be able to stand knowing you're here without checking you out for himself. He has to know what's going on in everybody's life. That's how he works in his parish." Walt shook his head and said decisively, "I don't need to know that much until there's something I can do about a problem."

Well, I thought, guess we'll see.

It was a busy time. We were already in Advent, the kids were starting in a new school, we were trying to learn the life of the parish and get enough unpacked so we could function. (When we moved, almost 16 years later, there were still boxes we hadn't opened.)

They eventually built us an office attached to the church, but at the start our office was in the parsonage. I was home alone one morning, unpacking, and I heard a knock. I went to the back door, which was the door most people used, and there was no one there. I couldn't see a car, so I assumed the visitor had parked in the church lot and come to the front door. I hurried around the corner of the house and saw a tall man, about my age, already walking away. I called out, and he turned. He had an amused smile, and he was smoking a pipe. "Hi," he said, coming back, "I'm Pastor Ken Losch."

And that was my first sight of my mentor and guide, the one who would light my path, school my thoughts, and offer my spirit a refuge whenever I needed one.

From time to time, the church tries to formalize relationships like this, assigning new pastors a more experienced nearby pastor as a mentor. This isn't a bad thing; if nothing else, it's good to know the people around you, for many reasons. But it's a bureaucracy's solution to a spiritual problem. You don't need just any guide on a journey like this: you need *your* guide. I was lucky to find mine knocking on my door.

We were both from Chicago, and we probably both liked to pretend to the rural folk that we were tougher and more streetwise than we really were. Someone told me once we were the two most cynical people he had ever met. I would give myself the edge on cynicism, but I would say Ken was clear-eyed. He was never blinded by how he wanted things to be or thought people should be. For some of our colleagues, that would come across as cynicism.

Ken taught me to see what was right in front of me. I was in his office once, worrying over something that had someone angry and agitated. He listened, nodding, then said, "Yeah. There's a problem there." Then he leaned toward me. "But it's not *your* problem. Don't start assuming everybody's anger is your fault." On another occasion, he told me: "Look: wake up. It's not that you can't please this guy. It's that he's unpleasable." (That single phrase was a gift that, fairly or not, often guided and consoled me.)

He liked to point out, in his down-to-earth, deflating way, that pastors have a bad habit of thinking themselves the center of the universe, for good or ill, taking both the blame and the credit for things that usually had nothing to do with them.

He was better at getting things done without friction than anyone I know. He had patience and took a lot of time to lay the groundwork for things he wanted to happen. He had an effortless connection with people, and he really did know a lot about his community. We were talking once about the habit church councils have of reporting complaints while refusing to reveal who made them. He said he once had a meeting in which almost every council member reported the same complaint; it seemed the entire congregation was enraged.

No one would mention a name, so here's what Ken did: he told them he'd write two names on a piece of paper and hand it around the room; he wanted to know how many other people, besides the ones on the paper, had complained—no names, just a number. He handed the paper around. It circled the table and returned to him in an increasingly embarrassed silence.

Saint Ken

No one had heard it from anyone else. What seemed like a congregational crisis was an issue limited to two individuals, notorious malcontents.

To do something like that, you have to be secure and calm enough not to get defensive and start arguing the issue before you know how big the problem is; you have to have a good enough relationship with the council for them to trust your instincts and your judgments; finally—and this is the hard one—you have to be able to come up with those two names.

I'm trying to illustrate how canny he was about the dynamics of a church community, but the real gift to me wasn't his example or his inspiration, but his presence, the ready welcome when I was feeling bruised, the ready wisdom when I called looking for specific advice for a specific situation.

Ken was a great defender of ordinary pastors and the ordinary life of the church. He hated hearing the synod staff talk about churches being in "survival" mode; he thought if a rural church was surviving it was doing well. He hated seeing articles in church magazines that praised attention-getting innovations, like baptismal services done in hot tubs; he loved declaring that a ministry devoted to faithful preaching, teaching, presiding at the sacraments, and visiting would never get you a write-up: it would only enrich your congregation.

In general, he thought most of the agitation for change and novelty that marked the time of our church service was silly and beside the point, leaving the real tasks of ministry at best untouched, at worst ignored.

We were driving to a meeting one day, and he told me someone had just finished chewing on him for being stuck in a rut, always wanting to do the same thing, always looking for reasons not to change, ridiculing every new idea as thoughtless.

"And you replied?"

He smiled wickedly. "I said, 'Yeah, okay—so what's your point?'"

Alas, one of the crosses he had to bear as the pastor of a large church with a large budget that it liked to spend on itself was having to put up with full-time, professional church musicians who loved elaborate liturgies and modern music. I'd often hear from him how unreasonably long the choir anthem was. "Nine minutes! Who in their right mind wants to hear a nine-minute anthem!"

Once, when we were on vacation, we worshiped at Ken's church: the choir loft was in the rear of the church and, during the anthem, the congregation mainly watched Ken craning his neck to see if it was wrapping up, sighing theatrically, looking at his watch, and shaking his head. He was so furious that day about the time the service was taking that he couldn't deliver his own sermon. While he preached, he kept looking at his watch and grimacing. (I liked telling people he was the only pastor I knew who criticized the length of his own sermons *as he preached them*.)

And yet he liked to point out how much his musicians contributed to community life, and he always defended their budgets. He was a ferocious champion of his entire congregation. Here's a story I heard from a couple of people, one of them Ken himself:

There was someone dying painfully of cancer, dying young, in one of the congregation's families. But the family had several active members in different churches, one of them in the local Assembly of God. The Assembly pastor had come around and, after assessing the situation, declared that the real problem wasn't cancer but lack of faith. If the family had even a little faith, their prayers would have been answered long ago and the cancer would be gone.

When Ken heard about this, he went home and got a baseball bat. He was coming out of the house to use it on the other pastor when his wife stopped him and stood in front of him until some of his rage drained away.

I don't know what the Assembly of God thought about that story, but the Lutherans loved it. I'm also not sure how exaggerated the details had become before I heard it, but, as we say about many legends, there's a good reason a story like that was told about this guy.

Ken loved the church. I think sometimes his family had to force him to take vacations. He told me that his wife kept pointing out that the church had lasted almost two thousand years without him and could probably still hang on for a week or two in his absence. Still, if a death in his parish occurred while he was gone, he'd often fly back for the funeral.

He was the head of the synod's candidacy committee and had an encyclopedic knowledge of every ministerial candidate's file. He got me on the committee, and then, when my term ended, kept me on as a "consultant." He had nothing but scorn for people who didn't take the job seriously and would just as soon have handpicked the entire committee.

The first half of my service as a pastor was graced by Ken's presence. I see myself driving with him, sitting in meetings and study sessions with him, walking out of the annual synod convention with him to smoke our pipes together. (I think we were among the last smokers to quit.)

Saint Ken

Then one day he woke up and couldn't use his arm. Then he started to lose his speech. A blood vessel had burst in his brain and a lot of us suddenly lost all the days and all the things we didn't even know we were counting on.

I think I first heard about this from Gary, another pastor in our conference, who called me after making a hospital call in Fargo. He had seen Ken in the hospital, thought he was making a visit, then realized he was being admitted.

They operated the end of that week. No one could really be sure how much or how little he'd recover.

The bishop, who should have come up and taken the service at Ken's church that Sunday, somehow decided he had other things to do. I took it. (The sermon I preached that morning can be found at the end of this book.)

One of my most vivid memories from my service is of sitting in that chancel before worship, listening to the prelude, trying to keep myself together. It was a big place with a high ceiling, and I seemed to myself unusually small. I really didn't want to be there. I remember marveling at the strange twists of life that had brought me to that moment. I remember wondering how on earth I ended up doing what I did.

But, at times like that, everybody in the room wants you to get through it well and wants to get through it with you—and you all do.

Ken survived the operation, came back maybe a little better than the surgeon implied he would, maybe a little worse than everybody hoped. After a couple of years, he retired on disability.

I'd visit him at the hospital when he was in rehab. When I left, I'd sit in my car in the parking lot, pound on the steering wheel and scream.

PART TWO

The Woman in the Window

You knew people in funny ways. In a small town, you were always defined by your office, so you met people from the start as your parishioners or not your parishioners. Factor in the multiple, crisscrossing family ties of a long-settled farming area and every relationship began with a shape well past changing.

We lived right across the highway from one of our parishioners, a pleasant, elderly lady. After not too many years had passed, we did her funeral, and her house was bought by a young couple with one child who had moved into town. But Angie, the wife, was the daughter of another parish family. For her it was a matter of moving back to the town she grew up in. Soon she was one of our Sunday School teachers, eventually taking a turn as its leader.

She might never have left. I was never sure I got the whole story of why her new family had returned to her hometown rather than somewhere else, but it was as though her interlude away had been erased. Even I thought of her as the daughter of Marie and Peter, an active volunteer in the church she had grown up in.

She became my personal hair stylist. One Easter morning, she pointed out that she had a lot of opportunities to study the back of my head during the service, and she had decided she could do a better job cutting my hair. She would do it for free, as a gift to the pastor.

She was actually an outstanding hair stylist, though glacial in her work tempo. I'd have to set aside at least an hour for a haircut, but I've never fought less with my hair than when Angie was cutting it. She was bright and fun to talk to. I got to know her well.

I have three strong memories of Angie, two of them appropriately church-related.

I could see her house from the church office. One day, soon after we had decided to accept a new call, I saw her walking over to the church and I thought I'd mention to her that we were going to move. So, when she came in the office, we had a little conversation about Sunday School and then

All Hands Stand By to Repel Boarders

I said, "Hey, I wanted to tell you: we got offered a call at another church, and we think we're going to take it. We'll probably be leaving in about two months."

Here's what she did: she looked at me with that vacant look people get when they have been captured by some sudden worry, some distant thought; then she stood up without saying a word and walked out of the room. I watched her leave the church, cross the highway, and enter her house without ever looking back.

She told me, days later, she just couldn't process what I had told her at the time. But, once again, I wasn't sure I was getting anything like the whole story or even if there was a clear story to be given. It was one of the many times I had to reflect on how little I understood about someone.

Our leaving also provoked my second church-related memory of Angie. There's a lot of handing over to be done when you leave a congregation, bridges started for the next pastorate, things to keep going. We must have been discussing Sunday School again and I must have thanked her for a job well done.

She said, "I was always terrified that you'd think I was stupid, so I worked overtime getting ready. I know what you think about stupid people, and I didn't want you to decide I was one of them."

I'm not sure how everyone would take that remark. I don't think I tried to make people feel like that. But I have to admit I was pleased that someone did. So I remember it as a compliment, if an odd one.

But the memory of Angie that comes to me most often doesn't have to do with the church. In fact, it's not one I'm involved in at all, except as an observer. It's a memory that's become for me a symbol of the life we all lived in that isolated little place.

I was out in the yard alone late one night, in that star-filled darkness that came down so completely around us. I can't remember if I was coming in from an errand or going out on one. It could have been a night I was out trying to pick out the constellations. I know it was winter because it was very dark very early and there was no one around. I happened to look across the street.

There was Angie, looking out her living room window. The window was open a little. She was smoking, blowing the smoke outside. The room she was in was dark, but there was a light further back in the house.

She was motionless, except for the hand holding the cigarette, but her head was turned slightly, looking down the highway. I watched her; she looked down the road. When I got cold and went in, she was still there, wrapped up in whatever her gaze was bringing her. After that first night, I saw her there often.

The lonely pose of that figure in the dark window always comes to me when I think of the life we lived up near the border. I think of the yearning that can swallow you in all that isolation, yearning for something more or just something else, something unknown you can't even picture in a wish or dream, yet you want it with all your heart. I think of people desperate to leave, people shipwrecked so they have to stay, people who came back stunned from finding nothing, people trapped by money, by love, by good nature, by bad choice. I see them all looking down the road, yearning.

Those are my thoughts, of course. I was always going to leave and I'm never going back. But I was there long enough to know I'm not the only one who felt that way.

Occupational Hazards (1)

It's sometimes hard to find things out in small towns because everybody assumes you know everything worth knowing already. Most directions you get are some variation of "Well, it's just down the *way*," spoken as impatiently as possible. More elaborate directions usually require you to recognize landmarks that have been obliterated for decades.

People calling on the phone—not, to be fair, anyone's favorite way to communicate locally—would never tell you who was calling. They would just begin talking, assuming you would recognize them and know what they were calling about as well. I could sometimes be wildly, hilariously wrong about this.

But one night the phone rang when it was almost midnight. I would get an immediate rush of apprehension and alertness when this happened. I jumped up and grabbed the phone. "Hello—Strugs."

I heard a woman choking, wheezing. She managed to gulp out, in a high-pitched voice that was almost a shriek, "You've got to come over! I called the ambulance! He fell down and I can't get him up!"

This was one of the many times I felt the Holy Spirit must be guiding me because I could almost see her getting ready to slam down the phone and I shouted, "Don't hang up! Tell me who you are!" It was an older couple I knew who lived only a block or so away. If I hadn't known where they lived, I don't think I could have gotten coherent directions from her.

When I got there, the town's first responder had already arrived and the EMTs and the ambulance weren't long in coming. I knew the woman who had called as a very commanding, self-possessed person: it was one of the first times I saw how shockingly and quickly the fear of losing a spouse can make someone come apart. She rode in the ambulance; I followed to the hospital.

This was one of my long hospital vigils, when I sat with two people, one struggling for life, one terrified, hour after hour, with not much to do beyond waiting to see if the next gasp for breath will come or not. That night, the breath came, then the breathing eased and, about five in the morning, we felt we could stand down and get some rest.

But, if you serve in the same community long enough, you'll watch all the old ones die, the strong elders who ran everything when you first arrived.

It's terrible to see a wife or a husband gripped by the first wave of mortal fear for their partner: you feel like an intruder—or someone granted an undeserved privilege you could never earn or be worthy of that's just thrust upon you. It's like stumbling upon nakedness: you feel you've violated something, crossed some forbidden barrier, and it doesn't matter that you didn't mean it.

It was always easier if someone else made that first call to summon you: you could get more information and usually get it more clearly.

One Saturday morning, we got a call from the daughter of a couple we knew and liked very much. They were active leaders in the church, not yet at retirement age, and the kind of patient, thoughtful leaders everyone should be thankful to work with. We knew them, too, because they'd already had their share of horrors: most recently, the husband had barely survived a severe farm accident and was still suffering its effects. (We learned, several years after we left that parish, that he died in another ghastly accident. Thinking about these two wonderful people and what they met on the earth is one of the things that keep me from seeing much sense in life.)

That morning, the daughter told us he'd apparently had a seizure that triggered a kind of violent flailing about. Her mother had finally restrained him with a neighbor's help.

This is one of those experiences where my memory comes in bursts: I remember the girl on the phone; then I see the hospital waiting room I'm walking into: the wife is covered in blood, I walk to her and she hugs me.

I don't remember anything I say or do or how long I am there.

My next memory is of me at home later in the day: I'm lying on my back in front of the television. I know I had no energy beyond what that took, but I remember I was watching the Michael J. Fox and Joan Jett movie, *Light of Day*. There was a scene in a hospital, and the camera was moving slowly forward down a long corridor.

Here's my last vivid burst of memory: I realize, when my head bumps the wall behind me, that I've been crawling backwards without knowing it, trying to keep from being pulled down that corridor.

Something in me that was deeper than thought must have feared I was being swallowed up.

Visiting

I somehow wandered into a retired pastors event a while ago, and the bishop had us all brainstorm about the advice we'd give new pastors. Someone said, inevitably I suppose, "Visit every member of your congregation as soon as you arrive." Heads nodded around the room. Not mine.

I knew somebody that did this. It was a large parish and the visits weren't much. I know because I was in the yard when one of them happened. The pastor, whom I came to know and like a lot, leaned over the fence, said hello, chatted, checked his watch at ten minutes, and moved on down the block. Not much, but still: it was a large parish and he did it. Give him credit for that.

By the next spring, the congregation was holding a meeting to vote on asking him to leave. (It was close; he won, but left soon after.) So, clearly, this magic bullet of congregational bonding doesn't always create the community it's supposed to.

Here's another version: someone in a forum, a layperson this time, was criticizing "today's pastors" (gee, everybody?) for "never visiting" (oh, c'mon: never?). He had a quote from some "famous preacher" who claimed it was impossible to preach a decent sermon without making 1000 visits a year.

It's always fun to hear statements like that because you get the chance to do some easy math in your head and get a few laughs. Let's see—give him two weeks off a year (pretty unlikely for a senior pastor, but it gives us a nice round number to divide with). OK: 50 into 1000, that's twenty visits a week. The statement clearly implies these are serious visits—otherwise, why make it? (My own view is that you're not getting to 1000 unless you fudge the numbers and count dropping in on the quilters' coffee break— "Whoa! Chalk up ten visits in ten minutes!") Anyway, say a serious visit takes an hour. Again, I'd say that was short, at least for the people I visited. (Some of them only brought out the cookies after 45 minutes). But we're trying to give this self-congratulating braggart a break.

So twenty serious visits a week take twenty hours. But again: the implication of that statement is that you *go* somewhere, so you have to *get* there. Let's say you travel a half-hour or so (round trip) for each visit. (A pretty low estimate: this would defy the laws of physics in the parishes I served.) So you're visiting at least 30 some hours per week, at an absolute, probably unrealistic minimum.

But remember: this is a "famous preacher," so there's also time needed for preaching.

One piece of traditional wisdom I found to be true was that, for a good sermon, you need an hour in the study for a minute in the pulpit. So a fifteen- to twenty-minute sermon needs fifteen to twenty hours.

Right now, our famous preacher is at a minimum of 45 to 50 hours a week: and we haven't talked yet about council meetings, committee meetings, confirmation classes, adult education classes, presiding at weddings and funerals with all the preparation those things deserve, spending hours with the same person in a hospital or during some crisis, or any of the unforeseeable things that can come upon you and swallow your day. Oh, and we haven't counted the morning of the service when the preaching happens either.

I told you this would be fun.

Sweeping statements like this, especially when they're divorced from real settings, are silly to the point of being meaningless. Their only use is critical, as accusations, and you can get a room full of nodding heads when you speak them. "Not visiting" is an easy charge to hurl at any pastor. It will always hurt because good pastors are already beating themselves up for not getting to the people they need to visit.

But I think the most important thing that's wrong with these sweeping demands is that they ignore the concrete realities and priorities of parish life. "Everyone" doesn't need to be visited right away—some people, however, do, and those people usually need to be visited more often than others: the dying, the sick, the grieving, those in nursing homes, those bound to their own homes, those who are troubled in spirit. The important thing "as soon as you arrive" is to find out who these people are.

As far as the congregation as a whole is concerned, your best introduction to them is preaching and presiding well at worship services.

But let's think further about the accusation of "not visiting." If it's simply being used as a weapon, there's little defense against it. But if it's a real concern and has any substance behind it, it usually means you're not visiting someone in particular. So: find out who that is and visit. I took every occasion I could to let people know that I wanted to know who was in the hospital, who was homebound, who needed some touch of support, who needed to be checked on. I would thank people profusely for informing me and assure them I would rather hear the same news a dozen times than have them assume I knew already.

In other words, the first mistake pastors make about visiting is shouldering it alone as a professional task: it's part of congregational life, something we should do together, and we should work at getting everyone to see it that way.

But there are those who expect you to guess that they want to see you or need to see you, who think you always know when anyone is in the hospital. (We could have members in any of five hospitals within an 80-mile radius.) You usually find out, usually as a complaint, after they're released from the hospital. An older pastor told me to reply, "I'm so sorry you didn't tell me earlier so I could get there," which I think is good advice and helps us get where we need to be.

But it's also true, because "not visiting" is such a charged and easy accusation, that there are people who want to attack you that way. They won't tell you when they're in the hospital; in fact, they will tell their friends they want no one to know; then they will use your failure to show up against you. You won't get a chance to use the above comeback because you'll never hear about it. Everyone else will.

As in so much of parish ministry, you have to know this, then live with it. Making visitation a consciously shared ministry and making sure you deliver on the requests is all you can do about it. I would also be sure, after I visited, to thank again the people who told me of the need.

(I must note one more thing: some councils require a report on how many people the pastor visits. This is no substitute at all for the common ministry I'm writing about here. Not only are statistics easy to distort, they're empty even if they're honest. Suppose I visit those 20 people a week: now suppose they are all young, happy people I like, and that I rarely enter the homes of the old and troubled, the sufferers in the nursing home, those sour and bitter about the lives that have crippled them. The numbers look good, even spectacular, but it's a hollow ministry. Statistics like this are worse than pointless: they allow everyone to delude themselves that the leadership is on top of things.)

I used to visit an older lady who lived alone on the farm her two sons still worked. She lost the use of one arm, though she could still get around pretty well and was tough enough to insist on living alone. But her sons convinced her to move into town. She was on my regular list but, if I'd get wrapped up in things and not get over to her house for a while, she'd give me a call and we'd find a time when I could drop over and bring communion. I often wished, and I often had bitter occasion to wish, that everyone who needed a visit could be like her.

The hard thing about visiting is that it's a part of ministry that's uncontrollable: people go in and out of the hospital, they go in and out of nursing homes for rehab, they're shut in but they're not *that* shut in; young families with two jobs and kids in school live in motion; problems and crises and trouble come on no one's schedule. There may be people who really need to be contacted but who are impossible to catch. (There are people who don't want to be caught: try following up on a counseling session with a spouse who spilled every marital misery in your office but, since then, reconciled a bit and healed a bit and is now ashamed of revealing family problems. Good luck.)

The hard thing to get over personally is doing it at all, phoning to make the appointment or walking up to that door and knocking. I'm sure I'm not the only pastor who treasured the famous passage in Reinhold Niebuhr's *Leaves from the Notebook of a Tamed Cynic* where he describes walking past the same house two or three times before he can summon up the courage to knock. I'm sure I'm not the only pastor to pray the Lutheran Evangelism prayer: "Lord, please let no one be home." But, eventually, it becomes one of the parish rhythms, you know what to expect from whom, how the visits will go, how to keep track of your time, when you should break out your communion kit, when you should do something else, how to summon up the courage to make the visit you really don't want to make.

I got to enjoy making the rounds, I missed visiting when other things tied me up, but, for me anyway, it was always an unsettled part of my service. I always thought I could have gotten around more, seen more people, seen them more often, listened more attentively, spoken more wisely, heard what was unsaid, uncovered what was hidden, left sooner, stayed longer. I suppose that kind of interaction with humans in all their complexity will always seem rough and unsatisfying. It certainly does for me.

When I was leaving one parish and making my last visits, I got handed a judgment that often comes to mind when I think about visiting. It was from a lady in a nursing home; she was in a wheelchair and had a little difficulty speaking. Especially at first, I found her hard to understand. But I got better at it, just in time to hear this:

"You hardly ever read me the Bible. You talked too much. You didn't pray enough. You're just not much of a pastor."

There is no court of appeal that can rule on that judgment.

The Visited

My friend Judy's mother, Inga, lived in a stately old house at the very end of one of the dead-end streets on the west side of town. She lived with her second husband and her sister, and their household was one of my regular stops.

You could see in Inga the liveliness and the deadly charm that ran through every generation of her family that I knew. They were the most likeable, happy people, who always managed to find their way out of stability and into chaos, and usually managed to attract people to bail them out. We all shook our heads at the mystery, but they were all too enjoyable to ignore or abandon.

Inga's husband, Peder, had a philosophical side that gave him a little detachment on things, a good quality to have if you were married to Inga. He was a great gardener and was on the point of giving it up when his knees went bad as he approached ninety. He thought he was too old to bother with knee replacements. After a frustrating year of inactivity, he had the operations and went happily back to his work. He told me to tell everybody I knew never to think they were too old to repair their bodies.

Visiting them was always lively, since Peder would reflect aloud on whatever ideas for human improvement happened to be flowing through his mind, while Inga would add her own variations and then, with an effortless shift, she would lead the conversation and he would follow. Inga, a natural hostess, would also be handing around treats and calling for more coffee, an extra spoon, another plate of cookies. It was her sister Elsa's job to keep the table resupplied and to satisfy Inga's whims.

Elsa was a tiny, slightly bent, white-haired lady who hurried everywhere and shook a bit as she collected and carried things. I think, on some of my visits, she might never have sat down. One day, Peder was droning on, Inga was shouting for a butter knife, and Elsa, who had already been sent for a cup and saucer, started turning about indecisively while the cup and the saucer parted company, and I thought: I'm at the Mad Hatter's tea party, Inga's the Queen of Hearts, and the Dormouse is having a meltdown.

All Hands Stand By to Repel Boarders

They were a lot of fun to be around. In my time there, they sank toward incapacity, then death. But they still visit me, and they always bring their full table with them, and the party never seems to end.

It's a privilege pastors have, to enter homes in a way few other people do. I liked entering the different atmospheres. Sometimes it was like time travel: so much of the past was sitting right in front of you. The old ones I visited were the children of the twentieth century, and their heads were still spinning from the changes they'd lived through.

I visited a man who had been a hired farmhand his entire life, always living in bunkhouses, never marrying or owning much more then he could carry from farm to farm. It was a way of life gone forever, or until the machines disappear.

Two of the first men I visited were war veterans, one from each world war. The older fellow liked to chuckle about goading the British troops: he would tell them the letters of his American Expeditionary Force patch stood for "After England Failed." His most vivid war memory was of tripping as he came out of the trench for an attack: a shell burst in front of him as he fell, split his helmet and his pack into neat halves while just barely nicking his skull.

The younger man was a jolly, stout person who was in a wheelchair. He had been a chaplain's assistant and showed me his portable keyboard and altar kit. He was the first person I had to learn to get away from. He would never stop talking and would never complete a story: a detail in one would send him into another, then the same thing would happen again. He would never come back to his earlier story but would keep generating narrative paths to nowhere, like a postmodern novelist gone mad. I think I listened to him for two hours the first time I saw him: I finally just said "gotta go," and left. He waved happily and told me to come again. I did, but I watched the clock.

Another veteran I saw a lot had been one of the men exposed to the radiation from an atomic bomb test. But it was his wife who was the shut-in: she'd had a serious stroke when she retired and he cared for her round the clock, with gentle humor and uncomplaining effort.

I admired the determination and the courage it took to keep living alone, but sometimes I'd be on the edge of my seat watching a one-armed woman with thick glasses trying to boil water or a half-blind, half-demented man with a linebacker's build and a mean disposition trying to hit a mug with a stream of coffee while bellowing that he needed no help.

The Visited

There was a lady who grew so quiet I had to lean in closer and closer until, during my last visits, I must have looked like I was sleeping on her chest. When her kids were there, we all found ourselves whispering.

But I think the hardest visits were to those who had lost most of their hearing. My intern supervisor said he feared losing his hearing more than anything, because of the isolation it brought. You find yourself talking more and more simply, less and less overall. The worst times are in hospital rooms or nursing home rooms where there are other patients or other visitors. You feel like you're shouting, you're still not understood, you can't stop thinking about the other people in the room who can't really converse since you're drowning them out, yet you can't just sit there and stare at the person you're visiting.

But you can't let the difficulties keep you away: being there is the important thing.

My most frequent stops were usually the nursing homes: every place we served had a couple nearby with some of our members as residents. Our second parish had four of them within a twenty-mile radius, though most of our members were in the nearest one. Nursing homes were a nice part of my visiting schedule because they're on their own clock, and you can plan visits more easily than you can sometimes with people living on their own.

When my service began, nursing home populations were pretty varied, and some of the residents weren't in that bad a shape. But, as the years went by, more people were able to live at home, and the general frailty and incapacity of nursing home residents increased. In our early prayer services, we'd get loud singing and hymn requests; towards the end, we'd get our only good participation when we went into the Lord's Prayer.

Visiting the nursing homes and care centers, you spend your time in the twilight of life: you're with people for their last conversations, their last looks and steps and touches.

But, last or not, they're still human words, looks, and touches, and I enjoyed the spark of life I found there.

One happy lady from a very pious family had her share of religious icons around her, but what you really noticed were the pictures of Elvis. She was sure if Elvis had lived he would have sung nothing but gospel music, but clearly his more secular music had enraptured her.

Another man I visited, Clifford, had almost nothing personal in his room but his clothing. He was a thin, quiet man who was missing an arm and had a dent in his skull you could lay your forearm in. He told me once that if I ever had to work around farm machinery, it was a good idea not to daydream. He always seemed a little distracted but he was a walking encyclopedia of Minnesota history. Some days, when I was tired, I would drop in on Clifford last and ask him something like "How was the country around St. Cloud settled?" or "When did the railroad come up this way?" and he would smile, look into the distance, and tell the story. He told me one of his earliest memories was hearing the school bell ring and ring, and someone telling him that it meant the Great War was over.

But you had to watch them deteriorate, lose their mobility, lose their pleasure in life, lose their sense of the world. You know, when you meet them, that they're leaving the earth, but through the years they become your companions, and you can't believe you have to watch them die.

Towards the end of my service, one of the most likeable and compassionate women I've ever met, a retired teacher, beloved member of the community, went into an assisted-living apartment attached to our nearest care center with her husband. He soon died; then she grew frail and had to move into the care center itself. She was in a wheelchair. Then she lost her sight. Then she lost her hearing. She had no way of telling what was happening around her or who was approaching her. She'd be rocking in bewilderment. She'd whimper and cry out. She might scream if you touched her.

That's when the pastoral visit finds its purity.

On the Road

I LEFT HOME AT nine one morning to make three hospital calls. I was going to visit three men who needed a little more care than our local hospital could provide but who were all healing well and looking forward to coming home. So these were going to be routine hospital visits, but the men were in three different hospitals. I visited in Grand Forks, North Dakota, grabbed some lunch, drove down to Fargo and visited there, drove across country to Thief River Falls, Minnesota, picked up more fast food, then made my last visit. The last man was a bright, talkative person, feeling pretty well, and I was losing my energy, so I didn't end the visit as soon as I might have. Still, I didn't stay forever, but, when I pulled into my driveway, it was nine at night.

That would have counted as one of my normal days.

I loved walking around the small towns we served in, but the fundamental reality of life there was driving: there were times you felt you were living on the road. One of the bishop's assistants I worked with turned her car into a small office-apartment: books and food, boxes of files, clothes hanging on a rod over the back seat. Bishop Lohr told me that's when he caught up on his reading: on the long, straight North Dakota roads, he'd prop a book on the steering wheel. (I tried this, then realized I wouldn't live to see how the book ended.) A lot of our members who would have farmed in the old days might as well have lived in the city: they did a three-hour round-trip commute every day. (The difference was: they were never stuck in traffic. Their time was spent on distance, not waiting.)

You had to leave town for almost everything; the more we all drove, the harder it became for local businesses to survive. A deputy sheriff I knew told me he started a project on his day off and needed a part he could only get in Alexandria, forty miles away. When he got home, he found they'd given him the wrong part. He went back for the right part, returned, and found it was defective. He went a third time, got a replacement, then thought it was time to quit and have a few beers. But if an ordinary person is willing to drive 240 miles in one day—not for work, not for an emergency, but for a hobby—no local business has a chance.

This also meant: if for some reason you couldn't drive, you were more and more stranded. Older farm couples who had sold their farms and moved into town to be near the hardware store, the grocery store, the clinic, saw, through the years, the stores and the clinics close or relocate.

Older people told me they could remember when passenger trains would take them up and down the state, even down to the Twin Cities: now they could only get there by driving, and they were afraid of the traffic. I wasn't fond of Twin Cities traffic either, and I often wished I could park somewhere, anywhere, and take a commuter train the rest of the way. But unlike older cities like New York and Chicago, the cities and towns in Minnesota had grown up with the automobile, shaped themselves to its needs, like docile lovers, and it will be a while before they realize they've outgrown it.

Since our first parish was a two-point, we drove back and forth between the two towns several days a week. I drove it so often I could daydream the trip away and be startled when I arrived. I memorized the placement of all the mileage markers in case I ever got stranded and needed to calculate my shortest walk for help. (I hit a deer once and, when I reported it, the sheriff's office told me they'd never had anyone give them directions by the mileage marker before.)

We were always dodging deer, even moose. There's nothing quite like seeing an entire herd of deer appear in your headlights on an icy road, hitting the brakes, and going into a skid as you hurtle into them.

We always lived close to a US highway, and one thing Minnesota excelled at was keeping its roads clear. So getting on the road was hardly ever a problem. But no one could do much about ice storms, blizzards, or the deadliness of the cold, should you be stranded miles from any help.

During our first winter, we'd hear people talk about a blizzard called a "white-out," and it's one of those things descriptions can't really prepare you for. Imagine driving in the worst blizzard you've ever driven in: now imagine your worst enemy is sitting on your roof and he suddenly pours several gallons of white paint across your windshield. That's a white-out: a blizzard so thick and relentless that you can't even see the hood of the car, let alone the road. It really looks as though your windows have been painted over.

It's the weirdest, most frightening isolation, trapped inside that whiteness. You naturally slow down, but you're afraid to stop completely because you're on the highway and there are other vehicles out. (Truckers are not known for slowing down.) They won't see your lights because they can't see anything. But as you drive on, you realize: someone might be stopped in front of you. Most tantalizingly, it's always true that one more mile could take you into better conditions.

I usually went on with that hope. You might as well have your eyes closed, but you're still straining to see. You have no idea how fast you're going or, much worse, where the road is.

It helps to have someone with you, if only to keep you from freaking out inside that white cell. But one of the survival tactics everyone used was for the driver to proceed slowly while the passenger or passengers leaned out their open doors and tried to tell where the car was by watching the stripes on the road, if they ever became clear.

A pastor's wife told me she was doing this in one storm and gave me this iconic piece of dialogue:

Pastor: "Am I still on the road?"

Spouse: "We haven't moved in five minutes."

There are two car trips that I'll never forget: one engine malfunction and one near white-out.

Our synod office was in Moorhead, just across the Red River from Fargo. I was coming home from a meeting there, early one January evening. It was very dark already, and freezing. I had the heater blasting and the radio blaring. It wasn't a bad night for January, and I was about halfway to Grand Forks on Interstate 29. (As this was early in my service, I'll note that I still didn't have a cell phone.) I was looking forward to getting home, out of the car.

All of a sudden, three things happened: all the dashboard lights went out, along with the radio and the heater; my headlights dimmed to almost nothing; a high-pitched scream came from under the hood. I got an instant panic reaction: I felt like my head was coming off, like I was choking, like my heart was trying to burst out of me. I looked around. It was like the night had embraced me. The North Dakota countryside had never looked so dark, so barren, so deserted. I think I could see a few headlights on the other side of the Interstate.

I figured if I stopped I would never start again. I thought, further, whatever had happened under the hood wasn't going to be helped by anybody outside Grand Forks. So I kept going and hoped I'd make it, or at least get close enough for a few more people to be around.

That was a long thirty-mile drive. Every instant, I expected the engine scream to lapse into silence as the car coasted to a stop. But the engine kept screaming and the car kept going and soon I could see the welcome glow of Grand Forks.

I knew the town pretty well, and there was a good-sized auto repair shop on the south side. All I had to do was hit my exit, make a right at the top of the hill and then manage to get through, I think, one light before I made it.

I went up the exit ramp and sailed into my turn, ignoring the stop sign, lucky to have no one coming. The next mile or so gave me cause to reflect on God's proverbial care of fools: no one got in my way, the light turned green, and I made an easy turn into the shop, where my car lurched and died. The mechanic told me he could get me going in a couple of hours and asked if I would like a ride to a restaurant while he worked.

Many thanks to everyone, human and divine.

I was equally lucky on the other trip, this time with a working car but no visibility.

The roads we hated the most in the winter were the straight east-west roads. Our worst storms came down from Canada and, in open country with dry snow already on the ground, a good wind could erase those roads completely. When the gusts hit your car, you thought you were being hit by a truck. If the blizzard was bad enough, you weren't going to see anything.

I was making a visit in a nursing home that was only about fifteen miles away, but it was due east across some pretty flat country with only a few houses and trees to break up the flatness. It was getting a little late in the afternoon and the winter light was dimming. I was visiting a gentle old fellow who still had a lively spirit in his frail body, so our conversation was rolling along pretty well. I happened to glance out the window and saw that snow, which I hadn't expected, had already covered my car.

"Halmar," I said, "I gotta get out of here."

He looked out, nodded, and said, "Pastor, you better head for the barn."

It was a thick snow, with fat flakes. I cleaned my windows and started off. It was hard enough to see in town, but when I hit the county highway it was like staring into a void. The wind was rocking the car, and snow was driving across my path, almost parallel to the ground. The farther I went, the thicker it got, the less I could see. I was navigating by the dark shapes I could just make out on either side of the road, blurry patches of farm buildings, groups of trees around farmhouses.

We all hoped, at times like this, that someone would have driven before us down the road, leaving tire tracks that hadn't been covered yet. Those were the best guides for navigating in the storms. But the storm had come on quickly and, that day, on that road, I was that someone.

After a few miles, knotted around the steering wheel, I was getting that familiar, terror-induced cramp in my neck and shoulders. The snow seemed to be coming harder. I turned my windshield wipers up a notch.

A gust of wind hit the car and cracked off the wiper on the driver's side. Now, in order to see anything, I had to lean toward the passenger seat and hope I didn't overcorrect my steering.

The dark shapes I was trying to drive between seemed to be getting both dimmer and farther apart. I was terrified of going off the road and burying myself in the ditch. I edged away from the side, hoping I could go roughly down the center.

But I edged too far, crossed the other lane of the road entirely, and felt the car sliding into the ditch on the far side. Out the window, for all I could see, everything looked the same.

I really don't know why I didn't slam on the brakes or do something else equally stupid to stall myself or bury myself. Maybe I was too cramped to do anything but plug along as I had been. Somehow I kept my head, the car's slide leveled off, I corrected very slightly and I eased myself back on the road.

I remember realizing I could start breathing again, then realizing that meant I hadn't been.

After that, my blind, cramped drive eventually brought me back to the town I lived in. I drove to the gas station to share my adventure and see if Danny might have a replacement for my windshield wiper.

He didn't, but it was good to be off the road and in contact with humans again. There were always people in the station, playing cards and drinking coffee. Even in the worst storms, the locals would drive around just so they could talk about how terrible conditions were. I stayed there for a while and happily joined in.

Then the door flew open, and a furious delivery driver stomped in.

"I wish," he said, "I could get my hands on the idiot I was following here. His tire tracks took me right off the road into a ditch and right smack into the UPS truck that went off the road following his tracks from the other direction."

Everybody laughed. Danny raised his eyebrows at me, smiling. But I hadn't spent four years as a pipefitter without learning how to come back at something like this.

So I said, "You're looking at that idiot. And, buddy, I hope the next blizzard that comes you're the first one out there and you can see how good you can do."

Then he laughed, and we all cursed Minnesota weather with the weird pride of people who had to live through it.

Perspectives

When I was on internship, my supervisor was musing one day on how hard it was to sift out the truth in counseling. He said something I've quoted many times since: "There are always at least two sides to every story, always. But, every once in a while, those two sides are called 'right' and 'wrong.'"

At War with the (Christian) Family

In our second parish, one of the people I often met on my walk to church was the school administrator. Karl was a great walker and one of the few people I would see walking everywhere in town. He was often on our church council and I valued his presence there. Since he worked at the school, he not only understood why you might need to maintain office equipment but also was used to handling budgets without hysteria. He told me once that, after twenty-five years of dealing with screaming parents, no problem in the church ever fazed him.

I met him one morning on the way to another conflict. He was going to meet some parents who claimed one of the teachers had ridiculed their child's religious faith.

"Science teacher, I bet," I said.

"Yeah, it was."

"And the parents are members at the Assembly of God."

He gave me a puzzled look. "How'd you hear about it?"

"I didn't," I said. "I'm just used to the Assembly. They prime all their kids to be provoked. They're looking for a fight when they walk in your door."

When I first began serving, I would often hear older people say, "Well, all the churches are really after the same thing." They were communicating their own tolerance as well as letting me know where they might stand in any religious disputes I might try to provoke. At the time, I would agree with them happily, communicating my own tolerance and generosity of spirit.

By the time I retired, the politest thing I could make myself reply was something like: "Well . . . "—long pause—"we should be."

My adult life, especially the time of my service in the church, was marked by the rise of the so-called Evangelical churches. They stood for a belligerent, authoritarian, socially conservative brand of Christianity, marked—scarred, I would say—by the leadership of white southerners. I considered the entry of these churches into public life a reaction to the Civil Rights movement and the advances made by women, as well as a general recoiling from the modern world, not unlike the fundamentalism of other faiths worldwide. Anyone wondering why American public life became so polarized and so ugly need look no further than the involvement of these churches in politics. Certainly, Minnesota politics grew more divisive as these churches took over more of the Minnesota religious landscape. The narrow, uncompromising absolutism of their politics reflected the narrow, uncompromising absolutism of their theology.

Public school teachers I knew, especially early on, were bewildered by the constant attacks they had to ward off about science requirements, health classes, library books, movies. Every time they'd meet one argument, they'd get another about something else. But this was because they never got the real argument: these churches hated the modern world and feared having their children exposed to anything in it; they didn't want to improve the public schools but to destroy them.

During the Iraq war, the school board thought it would be a good idea to learn something about Islam, so they invited a Roman Catholic scholar of comparative religion, a nun, to give a presentation one evening at the school. One of our members who was on the school board told me later they had imagined having a nun give the presentation would mean the religious community wouldn't have any problems with it. (This is one more example of how consistently moderate officials underestimated the ignorance and intolerance of the conservative churches.) What inviting the nun meant was that the school board got to meet a Christian mob, out for their blood.

After the presentation on Islam was announced, the next board meeting was packed. Anyone trying to defend the decision was simply shouted down. Our church member told me he'd never been in a room with so many enraged people and that he seriously wondered if he'd make it to his truck without being beaten or shot. The board cancelled the invitation. The Methodist pastor wrote a letter to the paper which several of us signed, defending the board and denouncing the intimidation, but the damage was done.

At War with the (Christian) Family

I found, when I was teaching confirmation, that I was more and more warning my students not to be fooled by the label "Christian," but to test what the self-proclaimed Christians around us were presenting.

We were discussing once, at the meeting of the local ministers' group, some of the differences between the various denominations. The Assembly of God pastor hadn't said much but, as the discussion was wrapping up, he shrugged and said offhandedly, "We just follow the Bible, so we don't have your problems."

It's hard to respond to such bottomless ignorance.

Instead I'll draw it out a bit with an illustration. During the first year of the Iraq war, this same pastor was in the Fourth of July parade wearing a T-shirt that sported a pro-war slogan: "Operation Iraqi Freedom." Here's my categorical response: the most authentic Christian way to follow Jesus Christ is the pacifism of the Sermon on the Mount; I would accept, in a sinful world, the defense of limited uses of violence along the lines of the just-war theory as a legitimate development of the New Testament; but the unqualified support of something so unjustifiable as the invasion of Iraq can by no stretch of the imagination be considered Christian at all.

Agree with me? Here's my point: even if you don't, as this pastor clearly wouldn't, you can hardly say following the Sermon on the Mount is *not* "following the Bible": so we reach again the problem of Christian differences such leaders are blind to.

As the years went on, I became filled with so much despair about the Christian community, its comfortable embrace of greed and violent force, its bigotry and its self-righteousness, that I began to wonder if we didn't deserve to be outlawed for the good of humanity.

When the Harry Potter novels started to come out, the same predictable voices were raised in condemnation of them. An elementary school teacher in our congregation stopped us on a walk one day and asked if we'd read them; she was hearing so many attacks on them that she at least wanted to know what we thought. So we got the first one and read it.

Thus began a decade of absolute delight as we both followed Harry through J. K. Rowling's magnificent series. This was my judgment then, and it's my judgment now: I think reading the Harry Potter novels, like reading Dickens, is a pretty good way of seeing Christian values in action. Moreover, I often think young people would be better off reading Harry Potter than walking into a lot of the churches in America that call themselves Christian.

The Queen of Hearts in Paradise

I WAS SITTING, LATE one night, with Inga, the Queen of Hearts, in her room in the Grand Forks hospital. I'm not sure why I was there so late. It must have been a full day because I remember being exhausted. I was at that point where it's easier to keep going, to prolong the visit, to stay on the road, than it is to stop and do something sensible like go home. Also, I always found it peaceful to be in a big hospital at night: there wasn't a lot of bustling, patients were sleeping, the staff was quietly watchful. It was a good time to be with someone when all you could do was be with them.

This would be Inga's last stay. The next time we were together would be when I spoke the last words over her on the day of her burial.

I felt like I'd known her a long time. We had been talking, then we'd stopped, and I realized I was comfortable enough with her to sit there without saying much.

It was a strange moment: we were just looking at each other, smiling. I was sitting pretty close. She reached for my hand, squeezed it, sighed and said, "Tell me something."

"What?"

"No," she said, "I mean—just talk. Tell me something. Talk about anything, what you enjoy, where you've been, what makes you laugh. Just—tell me something."

So I talked, but I can't tell you anything I said. I remember talking as she smiled but, most of all, I remember feeling lifted up into a realm of grace, out of time, out of grief, out of pain, out of yesterday and tomorrow.

It was like the moment the tenth leper came back and thanked Jesus for healing him. It was like the moment the good thief spoke gently to Jesus as they died together. It was one of the moments the church would be dead without, one of the moments that keep faith and life above the dark.

Later in the night, she said, "Let's pray together now. Do you think we can say the twenty-third psalm by heart?"

"Sure. Let's do it."

In my sermon at her funeral, I confessed we missed one line: the line about a table being spread in the midst of our enemies. I said: we must have missed it because with Inga you always took happy feasting for granted.

What I should have said was: what we missed wasn't the point. It isn't ever the point.

The Great Thing

Since I always served on a staff or as a co-pastor, I never had to write and deliver a sermon every week while trying to do everything else that needed to be done. All honor to those who do. I often said, not quite jokingly, "I don't know how real pastors can do this!"

And yet I felt lost the weeks I wasn't preaching. Having the Sunday sermon to meditate on centered me as nothing else did. For me, it was The Great Thing. As every writer knows, when you're writing, that imaginative world becomes a magnetic field, and it makes everything you encounter in the so-called real world jump, one way or another. I found no better entry into congregational life than preparing the sermon, and no better way to prepare the sermon than letting it bounce off congregational life.

Someone once asked me how I expected people to remember everything I said, but that's a poorly focused question, in many ways. I saw my task as addressing a given biblical passage or set of passages. In our tradition, we have an established cycle of readings, so we don't pick each Sunday's texts: they're given by the cycle. Thus, if I was going to speak on the prodigal son parable, my hope would be that the parable would come alive for the hearers. I didn't expect them to remember what I said: I hoped they would have a deeper encounter with the parable itself. So it's about more than memory, and it's not about what I say at all.

For whatever reason, all my life, whenever I've had some project to do, all my ideas of what to do with it would come tumbling in right at the start: if I waited to do my planning or neglected what came to me in those first thought sessions, I would find myself groping among old ideas and stale strategies. So, typically, if I was doing the sermon, I would do everything I could to avoid knowing what the texts were until I could get to my desk Tuesday morning with a blank sheet of paper and a full cup of coffee. (Obviously, this doesn't always work—say, on Christmas or Ash Wednesday.) Then I'd just read through the texts and hope they'd spark stories, ideas, connections.

Sometimes, knowing what texts were coming, I'd start going off in my head on my morning walk, and I'd have to find a place I could stop and scribble notes. I would actually start to sweat if somebody stopped me on the way and I tried to listen to them while hanging on to the ideas still percolating happily on their own.

That Tuesday-morning brainstorming was my most important time with the sermon: if I missed it because of meetings, emergencies, or unplanned encounters, there was no way to replace it. I was left to plod toward whatever I could put together and hope for better next time.

When I took those first notes, what I looked for—what I hoped to find—was something so strange I couldn't understand it. If something jolted me, I assumed it would jolt everybody. More importantly, if something strange in the text did jolt me, most lifelong Christians had probably done their best to ignore it their entire lives, so it was worth concentrating on. And it's always the oddity, the thing that surprises you, the thing you yourself wouldn't think or say or imagine, that unlocks someone else's world for you.

On good days, I could get a half-dozen pages of notes and, on the best days, they would be like tumbling dominoes: something in the passage suggested a story, a reflection, then another story, another reflection; just as importantly, they came in a natural flow. Sometimes, on the very best of days, my first few pages of notes became my basic outline and the skeleton of the final version. But nobody's that lucky every week.

There were two more stages in sermon writing that were equally intense. Friday morning, I tried to shape all my stories, reflections, allusions and points into an outline. (I tried to leave this flexible, and it was certainly never detailed enough that I would risk preaching from it.) Then, Saturday, I did the actual writing. When I still smoked a pipe, this took me from ten in the morning until five in the afternoon. Then, sick from all the coffee and tobacco I'd used to delay the writing itself, I'd collapse on the couch for a nap. Once I quit smoking, I cut two hours off the time.

I wrote out every word I would say: every halting allusion, every apparent stutter, every apparent qualification and aside. I planned every pause, every gesture. I'd practice some of them in front of a mirror. That manuscript was like a musical score for me. I could do without it, I could memorize it, but I thought that was time wasted that was better spent resting or playing with the kids. Also, I found not having a manuscript actually hurt my concentration and delivery: I was concentrating on what came next instead of how to get it across. But this is a matter where you have to please yourself: what's important, at the final stage, is effective delivery, however you get there. There's no such thing as the best way; if your homiletics professor says there is, drop the class and find another one.

The Great Thing

I did my translation and commentary reading on Wednesday and Thursday. But, for me, they were a lower priority; if something in my preparation got cut because of time, the translating went first, then the commentary reading. Again, I'm describing, not prescribing. In my worst weeks, I tried at least to glance at a commentary, so I wouldn't be too much on my own wavelength. But I got the most out of my own brainstorming, so that's what I hung on to.

(I've tried to describe here my ideal week of sermon writing. Especially if you're the sole preacher, one week like that a month would be a blessing. The worst, the absolute worst, weeks are the weeks of weddings: not only is Friday night lost to a pointless rehearsal that lasts twice as long as it should and no one takes seriously, but Saturday is swallowed by the ceremony itself, preceded by hours of hysteria as everyone realizes they could have used Friday night much more productively, and then the dinner, to which you really must go and for which to begin you must wait hours. With great luck, you might find a regular churchgoer at the dinner you can sit with, instead of hundreds of perfect strangers who all assume you have nothing to do the next morning. Amusingly, we found that one couple considered inviting us to the wedding dinner as the payment of our fee. I really did laugh when I realized that, because, by Saturday night, all I wanted was to be done with it.)

There were some things I thought it was important to avoid in writing sermons and two pieces of advice I repeated to myself constantly.

Here are the things to avoid:

(1) In Storytelling. I liked telling stories and I told a lot of them: stories about family life, working the jobs I did, school struggles; stories from my reading and movie watching. Stories are one of the handiest human ways to think and one of the easiest human ways to communicate. I always hoped I could think of a couple I could use. But if I didn't, I didn't.

There was a storytelling fad when I was at seminary, which, at worst, would turn the whole sermon into a story and make *every* sermon be a story. To require this every week for thirty years would be a lot to ask of Chekhov, Kipling, or Maupassant. It's silly to hand it to students as an ideal.

But it's even worse to use canned stories, the kind you get in pulpit helps and generic collections. I've known two pastors who did this in every sermon I heard them give. Listening to them was excruciating, like watching lecturers with broccoli stuck in their teeth. I always thought one word about my own kids or parents was worth a million about the poor little match girl or the sad old pastor with no hope at Christmas who sees a stranger sitting in the last pew. One honest word about anything is better than those stories.

Also, it's pointless to drag in stories when the passage you preach on is a story itself, either an event or a parable told by Jesus. Yours will always be worse. I've heard sermons that were labored, thinly disguised retellings of the prodigal son or the good Samaritan, and the only interest in them (beyond discovering how slowly time can pass) is seeing how the details match. We have all, to our great misery, heard this done to the Christmas story. (If I could figure out some way to stop this, I would die happy.)

(2) In Ending. I think I spent more time on the ending of sermons than any other part. That was the fuzziest part of my outline, since I liked to be flexible as the sermon grew. Also, I wanted to avoid having a kind of standard ending. I liked to end with one last jolt.

One pastor I heard a lot in college always went into his ending by saying "And so . . . " Sometimes, when he wasn't quite able to state "so . . . *what?*" very well, the "and so . . . "s would start to pile up. No pastor should want the congregation to be waiting for this to happen.

But the pastor with the worst habit of ending I ever saw was actually not a terrible preacher. He had a very engaging presence and a connection with listeners most of us would envy. He always spoke from the floor, not the pulpit, and the first time I heard him he ended by walking over to the pulpit and picking up a sheet of paper with one of his poems on it. Very effective, gripping ending.

Next week . . . uh, oh, he did the same thing.

How many weeks do you suppose I wondered if he *always* did this? (He did.)

How many weeks do you think it took before that was all I was waiting for?

Now here are the two pieces of advice I repeated to myself every week, most especially the weeks I struggled to begin.

(1) The first I got from Fred Buechner's lectures on preaching, *Telling the Truth*. (Buechner's work was so popular when I was in seminary you would hear a lot of people trying to sound like him. Read enough of him and you would be fighting not to.) He said he thought the most important, most promising moment in the entire service was the silence just after you read the gospel: the congregation sits, you are about to begin the sermon and—for the only time in the service—nobody has any idea what will come

next but everybody (or almost everybody) has hope for . . . something. They have hope in its purest form, completely without definition.

The advice was simple and powerful, and I had it bound on my wrist and fixed on my forehead: do not waste that moment. *Do not waste that moment.* Take off into the sermon. You will never have that same expectant attention again. Grab it by the throat and don't let go.

The temptation here is to take the easy way out of finding a beginning by showing how pious you are. Here's the worst way to begin, a way I heard too often:

We sit, look up. The pastor says: "May the words of my mouth and the meditation of my heart be acceptable in your sight, O Lord." The pastor pauses; then, as several people mumble "Amen," says definitively, "Amen."

The pastor looks at us. We are, most of us, still looking. The pastor says, "Grace to you and peace from God our Father and the Lord Jesus Christ." Same pause, mumbles, "Amen."

The pastor pauses, looks around. OK, I think, last chance. The pastor bows and says, "Let us pray . . . "

I can't tell you what happened next because I usually started doodling on my bulletin.

(2) The second piece of advice I picked up from the autobiography of the film director John Huston, but I could just as well have learned it from the Acts of the Apostles.

Huston said that, after he had prepared, rehearsed, and had everything ready to go, the most important thing he did was wait. He waited until the first set-up, the first shot, came to him. If he could wait for that, everything would flow. If he didn't or couldn't wait, everything that followed was labored, forced, like pulling teeth.

I can tell you that isn't as easy as it might sound. That blank paper (or blank screen) can look like a bottomless abyss, and everything in you wants to put something on it so you can get done. But I would also say Huston is absolutely right.

We faithful would call that waiting for the Spirit. It's as true of sermons as of houses: unless the Lord builds, those who build labor in vain.

Looking Back on The Great Thing

One of the (expected) pleasures of retirement is being able to reuse old sermons when you are asked to fill in for a vacationing pastor. One of the (unexpected) pains is having to realize few of them are as good as you thought they were. I always end up rewriting them and, most of the time, I have to shorten them quite a bit. I've had to admit, reluctantly, that I probably did go on a little too long, at times, as I would occasionally be told.

I was also told quite often I spoke much too fast, from my first sermon in preaching class to one of those I've recently given in retirement. (The person who last told me that said it was the only criticism she could make of the sermon, then said: "But I liked how carried away you looked!") I really did try to control my speed, but I liked flying along on language and I always liked listening to rapid-fire dialogue myself. Anyway, I thought I was usually fitting the delivery to the content. So, clearly, this is a lost cause.

One of our older ladies who was planning her sister's funeral told the funeral director she wanted my spouse to preach at the service because she had listened to me for ten years and had never understood one word I'd said. Well, she *was* deaf, but I like to think her incomprehension had its roots in my approach to the sermon. I made a great effort not to sound like a lifelong Christian who took the truth of the gospel for granted. I tried to sound like someone who couldn't believe what he'd just read. I hoped, on any given Sunday, I could come up with something out of the ordinary.

Driving back, not that long ago, from a supply preaching engagement, I was thinking about some of the nonchurch writers and performers that influenced me, especially stand-up comedians. I loved watching the old Steve Allen *Tonight* show, and what struck me about the comics was how completely they could captivate an audience, how tightly they could hold its attention. People who couldn't listen to a serious speech for two minutes will hang on to a good comic's every word for ten, fifteen, twenty minutes and not know where the time went. I liked the way comics would go in and out of character by just doing it, the way they moved from topic to topic in an easy flow. I liked how aggressive they could be with the audience. I saw how outrageous they could get away with being, as long as they were making people laugh.

From a theoretical point of view, I was very influenced by writers who were blurring the difference between high art and pop art—Leslie Fiedler, Pauline Kael—and I deliberately tried to make the sermon a rougher, more demotic, more jagged-edged, less pious, more surprising thing than people were used to.

That was what I wanted to do and I guess I was reasonably satisfied with what I did. (But, then, aren't we all? Let's say my feelings are least mixed about this part of my service.) I thought it might be of some interest to print the sermon I had given the morning these thoughts occurred to me. It can be found at the end of this book. (Note: the section where I'm asking the congregation what they want to hear in church is something I modeled on—or, well, stole from—Robert Donat's speech to the political meeting in Alfred Hitchcock's *Thirty-nine Steps*: "That's the kind of world I want! Is that the kind of world you want?")

My Desk, and What I Had There

We shared a desk in the parish office, but each of us had a separate work area at home. There was the desk I made my own. I loved working at it. I felt peaceful there, restored. It was where I wrote my sermons when I could, and I usually could. Here are some of the things I had around me:

Just above my head, there was a drawing of the owl of Minerva, perched on an open book, encircled by a Latin inscription: *studio et vigilantia*. There was a charming English translation with it:

> By Studie, and by Watchfulnesse,
>   The Jemme of Knowledge, we possesse.

I had pictures of people I admired: Ernest Hemingway, John Lennon, Virginia Woolf, Sam Peckinpah, Orson Welles, Audrey Hepburn, Dmitri Shostakovich, Martha Nussbaum, Bill Mauldin, the Rolling Stones, Thomas Eakins, Angelina Jolie blasting away with a shotgun, others, others. There was no special ranking, order, inclusion or exclusion: just pictures I happened to come across.

I had six typed quotations:

1/ *Niccolò Machiavelli:* When evening comes, I go home and enter my study; at the door I discard these daily clothes full of dirt and dust, and put on regal and curial robes, and thus condignly clad I enter the ancient courts of ancient men, where I am received by them lovingly, and partake of that nourishment which alone is mine, and for it I was born. Then I am bold to converse with them, and question them as to the reasons of their actions, and they out of their courtesy willingly answer me; and during those four hours I am above any trouble, I fear not poverty, nor does death appall me; I utterly become one with them. . . .

2/ *Karl Jaspers:* . . . contemplation and laziness are the sources of all good ideas . . . that meditative tranquility from which everything of intellectual value comes.

3/ *William James:* . . . to be a real philosopher, all that is necessary is to *hate* someone else's type of thinking . . .

4/ *Ernest Hemingway*: There are some things which cannot be learned quickly, and time, which is all we have, must be paid heavily for their acquiring. They are the very simplest things, and because it takes a man's life to know them the little that each man gets from life is very costly and the only heritage he has to leave.

5/ *Samuel Beckett*: All of old. Nothing else ever. Ever tried. Ever failed. No matter. Try again. Fail again. Fail better.

6/ *Pauline Kael*: The lowest action trash is preferable to wholesome family entertainment.

All these things look down on me still.

These faces and words defined, from the side of human aspiration, the spiritual landscape that I worked in, that I tried to earn a place in, week after week.

Fearless Moral Inventories

Almost everyone knows about the twelve-step program of Alcoholics Anonymous, but it would be a challenge for most non-AA members to name any of the steps in the program. If pressed, some could probably come up with something like yielding the control of your life to a higher power. But most pastors will be familiar with the fourth and fifth steps: 4/ the making of "a fearless moral inventory" of yourself, enumerating in detail all your failings, your misdeeds, and then 5/ the admission to God, yourself, and another human being the "exact nature" of your wrongs. That is, you actually have to tell someone, out loud, all the wrong you've done.

Most pastors, at some time, for someone, will be that other human being. It's not required that the admission be made to a pastor; but there's an expectation of confidentiality in this encounter, and it may be more natural to expect this of a pastor than of your uncle Pete. Also, you may not know anyone you trust enough to bare your soul to. If you're a long-term alcoholic, you may only know other alcoholics and people who no longer have patience with you, or hope for you.

In addition to confidentiality, there's also an expectation that the fifth-step admission will be accepted for what it is: a step along the road to recovery. It's not a time to express surprise, horror, or judgment. At this stage, the alcoholics are judging themselves. They aren't getting off easy. But, in any case, you can hear some hair-raising things and you have to be able to hear them calmly and compassionately, without reacting in shock.

Most of the fifth steps I was involved in were with people I had never met before. This didn't surprise me, because in rural areas the church tends to be seen as one of the bulwarks of society: it's part of the charade the decent people play at, and they make sure everyone knows it. This is a twisted fate for the disciples of the crucified one, but there it is. So people didn't want their own pastor to hear their stories: they'd call someone in another town.

Fearless Moral Inventories

It was important, when you got this call, to act on it immediately. I'd find some time when we could be free of interruptions and nosy people. I'd offer to begin with prayer or even to put the session in the context of a private confession: I had some takers, not everyone. But it's their show: I'd be quiet and let them go through their moral inventory, admitting to me, out loud, all the horrors and misery they'd caused by their drinking. Sometimes, once started, they'd talk for hours without stopping.

It's quite an experience to be that other human being. You see something almost no one on earth sees: guilty human beings revealing, not hiding, themselves. Not being chased down, not being confronted, not being accused, but freely accepting all the guilt. You see people who are no longer trying to look good but trying, with all the courage they can dredge up, to show how bad they are, how much hurt and harm they're responsible for, some of it beyond mending.

You see them walking through their own wasteland and, depending on how much wreckage there has been, there might not be much for them to hope for, beyond not causing any more harm. You see people headed up from the bottom, and it's something to see.

I look back on those sessions as some of the most courageous acts I've ever witnessed.

Fred and Ginger

At one time we started getting a lot of calls about fifth steps, much more than usual. Apparently, one of the county judges, impressed by the success of AA, had started requiring participation in a twelve-step program as part of the sentence or as a condition of parole, if there had been any substance abuse involved in the crime. Since there usually was, the local AA groups found themselves filling up with new members. But, since most of them were there unwillingly, some of them with undisguised scorn for the program, without the moral shock and desperation of hitting bottom, the recovery rate was going to be nowhere near what the judge expected. It was a way of seeing the difference between the moral and the legal imagination. The county social worker, with his own history of addiction, shrugged when we were discussing this and said, with that cold but hopeful realism of the best AA pilgrims, "Well, if people think a little more and drink a little less, I consider that a victory."

It wasn't my place to follow the people I talked to through the rest of their program. Anyway, recovery can be long and have its own twists and turns. But some of the people I encountered at that time were so dismissive of the program, so adamant that most of what they had done had been someone else's fault, that I had little hope for them. The person that told me the single worst thing I heard related the act as though he were describing a spilled cup of coffee. Besides, he insisted, it wasn't his fault.

Then, one day, in the midst of this cluster of fifth steps, we got a call not from an individual but from a couple. More oddly still, it was a couple we knew, Fred and Ginger. In fact, their house was just across the street from the church. You could see their backyard from the front entrance.

They were part of a group of young and no longer quite young adults who drifted around the area, appeared and disappeared, lived in one run-down house after another, in one pairing or grouping after another. I always wondered how they managed to support themselves. Occasionally, you would hear of one of them being hired to do a little farm work or help out

Fred and Ginger

with a building project, but if that's the kind of work you're always available for, you don't really have any work.

My friend Danny, who owned the gas station, was my informal liaison with all the nonchurchgoers in the town. Anything I knew about Fred, Ginger, and their group I got from him, but beyond their names, a little background and a few family connections, I didn't know much. I knew enough to nod to them and sometimes, after I'd been in town long enough, I'd get a nod in return.

One miserable night, when I was driving back to town in a violent thunderstorm, with no houses, no other cars, and no help in sight, one of them named Donny, who had thick eyeglasses and always dressed in black, came stumbling out of the woods waving his arms. The only reason I saw him was because the lightning was so intense. I have no idea where he was coming from, what he was doing, or if he had any idea how insanely homicidal he looked in his black outfit with the wind driving the trees and the lightning flashing around him. Donny got in as though I'd had an appointment to pick him up.

He said, "Glad I could catch a ride." Nodding his head, he grinned with such ghoulish innocence it made me a little nervous.

I guess that's a way of seeing the difference in the assumptions people live with.

Fred and Ginger, to my knowledge, weren't always a pair. At least, I tended to see them separately. If you went to a good-sized college, you knew people like them. Fred was thin, quiet, shaggy-haired, affable. He'd stroll along slowly, tilted slightly backward as though he'd rather be lying down, a gentle smile on his face, easing his way through the world. Ginger was intense, with dark, straight hair. She was tall and walked with long strides. I'd always get a smile and a nod from Fred. Ginger went by me as though I were invisible.

The house they were living in at the time they called us had been owned, when we first came, by an old bachelor farmer who belonged to our church. When he died and the house went up for sale, I'm sure I was not the only one surprised to hear that Fred had bought it and that he and Ginger were moving in.

Some of the older, more pietistic ladies took it almost as a personal insult that they had to contemplate someone like Fred as they left the church. Fred spent a lot of time in that visible backyard, enjoying life as he saw it. It was actually interesting to me to see how much groups can communicate without direct speech. The ladies projected their disdain, Fred became more loud and outrageous, everyone pretending not to notice anyone else. The most memorable evening was a night in spring when the Ladies Aid meeting walked out to see Fred playing his guitar in the nude. I heard he played pretty well.

I had a hard time not laughing when I was told about this, but small towns tend to find their own levels of mutual tolerance: just enough ladies in the regular group managed to see this incident as the joke it was, and Fred had just enough sense to see he'd hit a kind of limit. Without anyone saying a word, the boundaries of peaceful coexistence had pretty much been settled from then on.

It was not long after this that I received Fred's call, wondering if my spouse and I would do the fifth steps for Ginger and him. I said earlier that people in rural areas wanted to maintain the charade of decent society and often didn't want their own pastors to know the depth of their alcoholism, certainly not its humiliating details. But Fred and Ginger were the exceptions that proved the rule, in the true sense of that saying: they weren't part of the church at all, and they didn't care what decent society thought. Once the judge required them to enter a twelve-step program, they called us because all they had to do was walk across the street.

I was surprised, however, at the crime that brought them before the judge. They and some others had been raiding the empty houses of farm couples who were spending the winters in Arizona. I was surprised at both the scale of the operation and the energy and ingenuity it seemed to call for, a level of effort I would have thought was beyond Fred, though maybe not Ginger. Also, while I could see Fred being familiar with local drug suppliers, I was surprised that he would have the kind of connections that could convert stolen goods into cash. On the other hand, they might not have solved that problem yet: they were caught with a garage full of what they had taken, and I heard there wasn't much unaccounted for. It might all have been one of those alcoholic pipe dreams that went one step too far.

I thought I had a good session with Fred for his fifth step: he seemed honest, candid, self-deprecating, pretty open about his life and pretty clear about the wrongs done, the harm caused, the people hurt. He was someone I had a lot of hope for. And I liked him: he was smart, funny, inquisitive. He turned out to know a lot about music and composed a little himself. He lent me a book about Jewish mysticism. He was just someone whose life had

Fred and Ginger

taken some odd turns and landed him in our isolated corner of the world. But then, so was I.

After that our lives returned to their own levels. Fred and Ginger came to some sort of accommodation with the law. Another thing I always wondered was how so many people I knew, having done what I know they did, managed to stay out of jail. I would run into them pretty much as I used to. Fred and I were now a little more than acquaintances, and we had a reasonable amount of jovial contact. Ginger still marched by me as though I were invisible.

Then, weeks, months, later, I was in my office talking to a salesman from the company that maintained our copy machine. He kept showing me brochures for equipment that would do amazing things; I kept telling him there wasn't a chance we'd buy any of them. Suddenly, Ginger was in the doorway, wide-eyed, frantic.

She shouted, "Cordell, you've got to come over! Fred has a gun and he says he's going to shoot himself!"

I can see Ginger in that doorway as though it were all happening in front of me now. I had never seen her so rattled.

I told her to run next door and tell my wife to call the sheriff. I rushed for the door.

The salesman grabbed my arm. "Before you go, could you promise that if you should buy a new machine—"

I guess I never realized quite how obtuse salesmen can be. I screamed, "Man, did you hear what she said? I gotta go!"

"But you *will* buy from us if—"

I can't believe I responded, but I fear I did: "Yes!" Maybe I never realized how polite I was taught to be.

I ran across the street. Usually, when the old bachelor was alive, I had gone in the back door, through a narrow hallway into the kitchen. But I headed for the front door. I don't remember this as a conscious decision, but my survival instincts must have kicked in: there was an open porch in front and a big picture window next to the door, so you could see into the house.

There was a sort of double room to the right, the living room leading directly to the dining room. Fred was sitting back there, to the right of the table, staring at me. I couldn't see the gun. I walked toward him.

"You don't know anything," he said. He looked at me the way a god might look at a defiant worm. "You don't *understand* anything."

It seemed like a good idea to meet his gaze. I nodded and said, "That's probably true."

I made it to the table. We stared at each other. I nodded to the chair in front of me, he shrugged, I sat down. That seemed to mean nothing was going to happen, and nothing did.

We talked. Fred made sneering pronouncements on life, I made understanding noises and cautious qualifications.

After a time, the sheriff arrived with one of his deputies. I think Ginger was there, too. The sheriff was a big, powerful-looking man, quiet, thoughtful, who could project an atmosphere of calm and order. I was glad to see him. He asked if it was alright if he had a private talk with Fred. We both nodded and I moved back to stand by the deputy.

As I've looked back on this day, I've sometimes wondered what possessed me to walk through that door when I knew Fred had a gun and was probably drunk. But I can't say I was weighing consequences: I was just thinking I should get there. I couldn't believe Fred would hurt me, but I can't say I consciously considered that either. As I probe my memory, my focus at the time seemed pretty narrow and concentrated. I was like an outfielder chasing a fly ball, not thinking about what he might collide with.

I also recall parts of this episode much more vividly than others: Ginger in my office doorway, the salesman stopping me, me crossing the street, then walking across that room and being told I knew nothing, the sheriff speaking calmly over my shoulder. Most everything else blurs. I'm not really sure that Ginger didn't walk in with me, though she had to have called the police sometime. I don't even remember going home.

Here's my last clear image, and it's a fitting chorus-like comment. I was standing next to the deputy while the sheriff and Fred talked quietly. The deputy sighed, leaned toward me and whispered, "Man, I cannot tell you how sick I am of being called to this house."

But, once again, our lives returned to what they had been. Fred and Ginger appeared as usual around town, Fred rambling, Ginger rushing.

I was in the gas station one morning, talking to Danny, when the two of them walked by outside, in their separate rhythms. Danny and I looked at each other and laughed softly. More communication without words. Danny was a tolerant spirit. He said, "You know, those two are really pretty good-hearted people." He thought a moment and continued, "They should just learn to stay away from alcohol."

When the Dead Awaken

Small towns in rural areas have lost a lot of what they had, but they've retained their cemeteries. People who grew up on the surrounding farms, even if they've lived elsewhere for half a century, will have their bodies brought home for burial. There are empty churches all over the countryside with perfectly maintained cemeteries, still the scene of graveside services. We did many of them, after performing the funeral itself in our own church. We would often get calls from distant funeral homes, announcing deaths, making arrangements. Once we got a recorded call that a body was on the way from Ohio, whose name no one but our oldest members could recall. Even they weren't sure what church his family belonged to, if any.

Sometimes our local funeral directors would handle the requirements, but sometimes, if they were close enough, an out-of-town funeral home would send up a team with the body, and they would assist at the services. We had one come up once at the death of an extremely old man. He had died in a nursing home in North Dakota and most of his family were already gone. Again, only our very oldest members remembered him. It was going to be a very small service, so the funeral home sent up a small crew, led by the son of the funeral director on his first solo outing.

We got along well, the service went smoothly. But, as we processed out, I noticed the young man was staring at the casket with a puzzled look, moving his finger in the air.

When we got to the hearse, he told the pall bearers to turn the casket in a half-circle. He stared at it, nodded, and had them slide it in.

But on the short ride to the cemetery—down the highway and across it—he got out a piece of paper and sketched our path in and out of the church. I realized he was trying to figure out which end of the casket the head was on.

Here's why:

When the Dead Awaken

Everyone in our cemeteries was buried on an east-west axis, with their heads on the west side, thus facing east and the dawn. (One cemetery was an exception: a community of Norwegians buried their dead on a north-south axis, facing north. If you know an isolated community of Norwegians, this will make perfect sense to you.) The idea seems to be that, when the dead awaken, they need to be looking in the right direction. Knowing where the sun comes up seems like a small challenge next to rising from death, but it's the only explanation I have. Anyway, it seemed to be important to a lot of people.

The young funeral director was still revising his sketch when we arrived. The line of cars pulled in the cemetery after us. We would have a little walk across the grass, and it would take awhile for everyone else to gather from their vehicles. The young man looked nervous as he folded his paper.

We got out. He collected the pall bearers and got them in position.

He said, "Please face the hearse. As I pull out the casket, grab the handles without turning around. Then we'll back up and turn toward the grave."

He pulled out the casket halfway, then said, "Wait." He stared at it. He was now looking very nervous. He pushed the casket back into the hearse.

"OK. Instead of facing the hearse, face me. Now: when I pull out the casket, grab the handles with your *other* hands."

Some of them literally looked at their hands, unsure of everything at this point. I hate to say I was enjoying this. But I was.

We started toward the grave. He stopped them again, thought, drew lines in the air, then had them circle the headstone, pass the grave on the other side and back up to the rollers that would lower the casket into the vault.

When I got home, I sketched my own map of the body's journey around the compass.

Should the Last Day of Time's Cycle bring anything like the event assumed by all our fussy burial positions, our area should reveal: several Norwegians facing north, most everybody else facing east, and at least one lonely pilgrim, who should have had enough sense to do business with a local firm, facing west.

Of Little Faith (1)

WHEN WE FIRST BEGAN serving our two-point parish in northern Minnesota, the church schedule was set by the dairy farmers and their schedules: evening meetings started after milking; Sunday service times were set so people could finish milking and get cleaned up. The red-brick creamery on Main Street had only recently closed. By the time we left, sixteen years later, there was only one dairy farmer left, and he would probably not be doing it long. A huge, industrial-like dairy farm appeared south of us, bringing all the environmental horrors our deaf, dumb, and blind government never seems to notice.

Moving to central Minnesota, we watched it happen all over again: creameries gone, farm families dwindling, farms themselves being consolidated, run by a handful of people.

There was a little town about every six miles along major roads, once an easy wagon ride in from the surrounding farms. They all had a grocery store, a hardware store, a bar, and a church. In the bigger ones, you might have a choice of bars and churches, and there would be a school. The buildings are still there, empty, like the sagging barns on the abandoned farms.

Most of us pastors were serving those tiny churches because the vibrant life of an earlier time had built them there. If you served in that area in the last decades of the twentieth century, you had a front row seat to watch that life die.

But you weren't watching something new, or unusual. Most of America's population, like the world's population, has been moving from the country to the city for a century and more. What I've set down here is a snapshot of a serious economic and social shift, but it's not the only snapshot and it was taken late in the game.

Here's a despairing joke I heard: guy goes into a hardware store and buys a dozen hammers for ten dollars each, then stands outside the store with a sign that says "Hammers—$9." Somebody asks him why he's doing that. Well, he says, I'm making a lot more money than I do with farming.

Of Little Faith (1)

The night I heard that joke I was at a Lions Club meeting, and I was sitting next to the man who had been managing the local hardware store when it closed. As everybody laughed, he muttered, just about loudly enough so I could hear it, but without looking up, "I wish they'd done that when I ran the hardware store instead of driving to Grand Forks for everything they needed."

Here's another joke. This one is typically told by the local businessmen, not very loudly, usually when no farmers are present: What do you call a basement full of farmers? A whine cellar.

Watching this life passing, I used to think about the Chicago neighborhood I grew up in: it was full of family-owned businesses: two drug stores, a grocery, dry goods, a bakery, a shoemaker who could barely speak English. They were wiped out by the same forces that were wiping out the farms.

I never heard a good word about unions from a farmer. They cheered when Ronald Reagan went after them. It never seemed to dawn on the farmers that the unions might be fighting their battle. At those times, I thought of Martin Niemoller's famous lament: I never said a word when they came for the others, and no one was left when they came for me.

I talked to one farmer who was outraged when Reagan wanted to cut farm subsidies. I wanted to ask him what he thought Reagan meant when he said he wanted to get rid of government welfare. But I knew what he thought Reagan meant. So did Reagan.

And yet there they were: people who really were losing a way of life, people you knew and loved. You couldn't see what was happening without wanting to be on their side, without wanting to do . . . something.

I sat in a lot of pastors' meetings where we'd worry over the state of farming and all our changing times meant. We'd have speakers who could recite every statistic and every trend imaginable, not only about farm employment but food itself, land use. I'll never forget one county agent, to his credit, going into a rant about the growing inequality in America.

At some point in these meetings, some pastor would ask: What can we do? Some pastor would beg: Tell us, tell us what we can do.

Meeting after meeting, I would sit there formulating an answer I never quite had the chutzpah to stand up and give out loud. Here it is:

"Well, as I see it, to really change things, we're going to have to overthrow the government first. It's nothing but the pawn of Wall Street. Once we nationalize all the corporations, we can sever their ties to the international capitalist community. Then we'll nationalize the farms, break them up into smallholdings, and drive the population out of the city and back to the country. We'll have to ban all large farm equipment so people have to use more laborers. Oh, and we'll have to ban the automobile, too, to force everyone to shop locally. Short of that—fuck, man, I don't know WHAT we can do!"

What we, in fact, tended to do was to keep repeating all the dismal statistics and trends and to talk a lot about stress and ways to fight it. I guess you could say we took on mental stress instead of capitalism, a kind of proxy war in which, like all proxy wars, local victories don't mean that much.

Here's what bothered me the most:

I would watch these pastors begging to be told what to do, begging to be given some useful task, and I realized that they saw nothing in what they normally did, nothing in what they spoke and sang about every week, nothing in the faith they'd given their lives to, that meant anything before a serious problem.

The gospel is full of things to do in the face of a crisis, any crisis, because the gospel is addressed to everyone, in every time and place.

Here's something to do: love the Lord your God with your whole heart, your whole soul, your whole mind and love your neighbor as yourself. No matter what shape you're in, you still have neighbors: love them. Believe me, you'll find someone worse off than you: help them.

Here's something else you can do: lay not up for yourself treasures on earth, where thieves break in and steal, and moth and rust consume, but lay up for yourselves treasures in heaven.

In all the meetings on these issues and these problems I attended, I never heard anybody say anything even close to: one thing you can do is sell all you have, give to the poor, and find some way to follow Jesus. (To be fair, we never say this seriously in church either.)

Sitting there clueless, the clergy revealed we all too often thought of the gospel as comfort, never as call, never as the great disturber of our peace, never as a summons to a life beyond getting, spending, enjoying.

Jesus didn't tell only the wealthy and comfortable to deny themselves and care for others: *he told his disciples, he told everybody,* to deny themselves and care for others.

In other words, we could do what the church has always been doing. We only needed to have faith in it. It's the summons of the gospel, turning from the earth to love God, and the challenge of the gospel, turning away from yourself to love others, that give people the backbone, the inner strength, the toughness of soul, to stand up to a crisis.

It bothered me a lot that what we seemed to want most was to help people be successful and financially secure. We came too close to speaking and acting as though mammon really were our true god.

PART THREE

Required Reading

There's a look people who don't read that much get when they manage to finish one of those popular inspirational books that are always appearing. The Apostle Paul must have looked like this when he first regained his sight. They rush to everyone they know to hand on the vision. Pastors who don't read that much are usually the worst: it makes them feel they're finally being active evangelists.

This in itself gave me a strong reason to avoid these books.

But I did have my own list. I used to say there were three books all pastors should read to prepare them for parish ministry:

1/ Niccolò Machiavelli, *The Prince*;
2/ Edmund Burke, *Reflections on the Revolution in France*; and
3/ Leslie Fiedler, *Freaks*.

Everyone would always think I was kidding.

Breakdowns

AFTER WE RETIRED AND moved, we were looking for a church we could transfer our membership to. We found one that seemed both lively and liturgical that we thought we could be happy in, but we had a hard time getting the pastor to talk about membership. He was about to retire himself but that wasn't the problem. He would disappear quickly after services and, if you did manage to snare him into a conversation, you had the impression you were something he had gotten caught on accidentally and was desperately trying to get away from.

The people in the congregation we got to know would roll their eyes about him, or worse, and claim he never learned anyone's name and could never recognize them outside church grounds. I took this, of course, with a grain of salt, knowing the gossip scene quite well. But I had also seen behavior like this before.

It was the behavior of someone deathly afraid of being attacked, afraid that any conversation would lead to the words "But, you know, there's something I really have to bring up . . . " So he made sure, by jokes, by deflecting remarks, by moving away and signaling he was overdue somewhere else, anywhere else, that no conversation could go on long enough to escape triviality.

The most extreme example I had seen of this was an old Roman Catholic priest, also nearing retirement, famous for his jokes and silliness, virtually unable to be still and know you were in front of him, wanting to talk to him. He could barely meet your eyes. He was running from serious contact every minute of every day, something impossible to do successfully as a pastor. Eventually, just short of retirement, he had a complete breakdown, was subjected to the most extreme treatment we've dreamed up for our wounded souls, and walked around after that like an empty shell, hollow-eyed, without, it seemed to me, either fear or hope.

Pastors can condemn themselves constantly, without anyone else's help. When someone else comes after you, the damage is magnified by your own sense of failure. When it's some issue you haven't thought about, some

Breakdowns

offense you had no idea you'd committed, you feel absolutely naked, sick from that sudden exposure. It takes all the discipline you have to be able to listen to the attack, hear what's being said, and then find a way to respond that doesn't make things worse. Hearing the attack secondhand, from a friend, is not much better. No one wants to have that conversation. Have enough of them and you won't want to have any conversations. Hurt badly enough, you will get the look I've been describing. Occupational hazard, but definitely a signal that it's time to go, like a radiation badge.

We had two long periods of service: in both of the parishes we served, we followed immediately or not very long after a pastor who was hospitalized because of breaking down. (I keep searching for a proper word: this is more than mental breakdown; it's emotional, spiritual; it's a collapse, a paralysis of life, a loss of that fragile ability to tie your shoes without thinking and get on with the day that most of us take for granted; a loss of happiness. You can't even remember what it's like to be happy. You look at thoughtless people laughing and you're sick with envy.)

But the two pastors we followed walked very different paths to their ends.

In our first parish, the pastor's small grandson had been kidnapped. Eventually, the boy was found to have been killed, but for too long the family lived with that unimaginable horror of the missing child. Always anguishing, always heart-wrenching, but add to the anguish the duty of getting up in a pulpit every week to speak the words of life. You must speak them to people who, to put it bluntly, have their own anguish, their own heart-wrenching pain, and not much time for yours. Add to your anguish the duty to visit the grieving and bring them the word of faith, to preside at funerals while wondering if your loved one is living or dead, and, if living, what is being done to them? You must baptize the newborn infants of happy parents.

Work and duty can be a saving distraction to a wounded soul, a call back to life. I wouldn't deny this can happen. But sometimes the work and duty of a pastor become nothing but salt in the wounds, a mockery and reversal of all you say and do, and it was so for this pastor. The story goes: He simply called the bishop one Sunday morning and said he could not physically step into the pulpit any longer. Please come help.

In our second parish, the pastor's life was assaulted not by the random, murderous act of a stranger but by the daily, grinding complaints, sneers, accusations, casual distortions, and relentless, sour gossip of the family, that Christian family that loves to sing about itself and its love.

Nothing even remotely comparable to murder happened to this pastor. For him to describe as problems one or two or three of the petty acts that ground against him day after day would sound silly, laughable. If he listed all of them for you, he would seem like the petty spirit, upset over trivialities. Sympathy for the daily grind would be hard to come by. Still, it wasn't one destructive act that broke him but the daily friction of petty, uncooperative people whom he could not please.

I'll give a clear example from my time of service in that parish, an example that didn't involve me. We were, as always, having trouble with our office copier. But understand this: there were vocal people in the congregation who thought we didn't need a copier, let alone a computer; when we bought one, it had to be the cheapest available; no one understood why maintenance had to be paid for. So our problems with our equipment were chronic, and our ability to address those problems was crippled by the resistance of the congregation.

One new council member thought he could help: the business he worked for was upgrading their copiers and offered to give us one of their old ones. Free. It was also delivered free. Unfortunately, it was delivered the day before the church quilters met at the church. The evening after they met, the council president got a screaming phone call from one of them, wondering how the council dared to buy a new copier when the church was struggling financially.

Let's first savor what that evening accusation implied: these ladies had seen the new copier, concluded what in their eyes was the worst, spread the story as far as their tongues could take it, whipped themselves into enough of a fury to attack the council president—all without anyone bothering to find out the real reason the copier was sitting there.

Note that the phone call was not about finding out why it got there: it was to attack the council for something which in fact it hadn't done. Note, too, the assumption that the council would have no right to obtain a copier, even if it had the daring.

This is a clear example on a fairly large scale of something that happened in this congregation week after week, year after year. I found out years later that, when the former pastor left with his breakdown, his wife wrote one of these same women an accusing letter, blaming her for what happened. Believe it or not, I was told that by the woman who got the letter, wondering how the pastor's wife would dare send her something like that.

Now, you might think such a clear case of being wrong about what was really a free gift would 1/ be easily waved away as a problem, perhaps be chuckled about over drinks at the Vet's club, and 2/ might make people think a bit about the other distorted gossip they heard.

Here's what actually happened:

I found out about the encounter the next day. The president at that time, my friend Rick, was a calm, reasonable person, one I would have trusted with my life. He also had a much more optimistic and generous view of human nature than I did. He shook his head about the phone call, and he laughed at how silent his attacker had got when he countered her with what had actually happened. He felt the pure satisfaction of knowledge triumphing over ignorance.

But he only corrected one person. The anger, the accusations, the relentless suspicion of the church leaders, were still out there simmering. It was highly unlikely the corrected person ran around correcting everyone else. I always thought, no doubt foolishly, that this was a wasted opportunity and that we should have forced more of a confrontation with whoever had cooked up the falsehoods.

But moderates in any organization are always slow to act and unwilling to act largely. If things get bad enough, they are more likely to refuse positions of leadership or resign from them than to take on the malicious members. It's the antagonists who never quit. That's the problem in a nutshell.

One of the most disheartening things about this episode, and perhaps the greatest missed opportunity, was that we never even used it within the council to define one of the congregation's great problems. Ironically, the young member who'd donated the copier was part of the antagonistic set and had come on the council as something of their standard bearer. I thought he should have been made to see that the distorted gossip his act had given rise to was only one more example of what the people he listened to were always doing, most of the time with just as little relation to the truth.

That I've carried on so long about this underscores my point: this wasn't even something I was much involved in, I wasn't the one being accused, and here I am raving about it years later.

But now: say a pastor is himself involved in several of these distorted assaults; say the council president at the time isn't that calm and reasonable;

say the antagonists are on the council; say, as I found out later, the pastor is told there is no money to pay his salary for weeks, then months.

Now the pastor must step into the pulpit to speak the words of life to the very people who are assailing him. He knows, all too well, that every word he says can be twisted into an insult. He knows this because he's already heard, many times, by roundabout report, that words he has spoken have been. He has also been told this is the reason attendance is poor and giving is terrible.

One of the funeral directors who served this area told me that, by the time this pastor had to leave, he was leading services in a daze and his funeral services would last only five or ten minutes.

I'll speak elsewhere of institutional responses to this problem, but I don't think anyone has improved on the two shields forged by the ancient world against misfortune, loss, and sorrow: the philosopher's detachment, and the believer's laying up of treasure in heaven, where moth and rust do not consume and thieves do not break in and steal.

In other words, to create that inner fortress, the rock on which the wise person builds, you should be as much like Socrates or Jesus as you can. I haven't seen this mentioned much in things I've read on the subject, yet I believe it's the best we can say. I also believe those two great teachers of life did not live in vain and that we can go some way toward living like them and, as we do, so we are strengthened and shape a character that can blunt the arrows of fortune.

But pastors are like everyone else: they want ordinary human happiness, that castle not just within, but out in the world, surrounded by health, peace, praise, respect, fulfilling work, reward for effort. Out in the world and, thus, vulnerable to attack, of every sort, and suffering, too, of every sort. Given enough of either, ordinary life becomes unbearable.

People That Drove Me Nuts (1)

There were always a few people on the church council who considered themselves budget hawks. No matter what we needed, or what it cost, they were convinced they could get it for less or, if not, that we could "get by" without it. If you've ever driven through rural America and seen barns with gaping holes in their roofs, their walls sagging to one side, boards missing, paint peeling off, you have an image of what my church council members meant by "get by."

We'd be discussing the bills that were overdue—part of being a budget hawk in the church seemed to require making sure no bill was paid on time—and one of the bills would be, let's say, for the service that brought us toilet paper and hand towels.

Scowling, head shaking, someone would grumble, "Too much. WAY too much. Look here now: somebody driving down to St. Cloud could pick up what we needed for half that. Less."

After several years of hearing this judgment and knowing that the likely follow-up would be that we would "get by" without the item in question, I would snap, pretty sharply, "Who?"

"What do you mean?"

"Who? *Who* is going to drive to St. Cloud and pick this up?"

Laughter at the obvious. "Anybody. Whoever's going that way."

"You?" I would continue pointlessly.

Rueful laugh this time, regretful shrug. "Well, I don't always get down there as often as I'd like. But somebody's always going."

I would sometimes continue, even more pointlessly, "Okay—so who's going to find that out and arrange it? Are you?" But after several years of the same dialogue, I knew continuing it really was pointless. No, of course, that person was not going to lift a finger to do anything but stop us from doing something we could do easily and force us to search for a roundabout, hit or miss, laborious alternative that would only save us money because the church would never reimburse the fools who finally agreed to "pick up" what we needed.

All Hands Stand By to Repel Boarders

There is at least one person like this on every small church council, but, at the church that brings this scene most strongly to my mind, it's no surprise that the council finally stopped buying toilet paper completely. They thought people would eventually be driven to bring their own.

People That Drove Me Nuts (2)

THE FIRST BISHOP WE served under, Harold Lohr, was one of the finest leaders anyone could ask for, and he had a standard piece of advice for his new pastors: when you begin serving a new congregation, don't change anything for a year. New pastors are changes in themselves, especially if they're following someone who served there for ten years or more, not uncommon in the old rural parishes. You should spend your time finding out who the people are, what they do and why they do it, what they love, and what they can and cannot bear losing.

When he gave this advice, he would finish by raising an eyebrow and saying, "All those great ideas you're bringing from the seminary might not look that great after you let them sit for a year."

I've had cause to reflect, over the years, that this advice might hide an assumption that pastor and congregation shared a great deal to begin with and, when I began serving, this was true: the same liturgical expectations, knowledge of hymnody, the same assumptions about Christian education, Sunday school and confirmation material. You could be—and we were, in our first parish—worlds apart from the pastor you followed, have nothing in common personally, socially, politically; but the crucial thing was whether you shared church practices. If you led the same liturgy, picked enough of the same hymns, and continued the education program along the same lines, you would be standing on common ground. You could build together from there. What has happened over the years, however, is that more and more pastors prefer to design their own worship styles and educational programs. Each new pastor, thus, has less common ground on which to meet the congregation: everything becomes a personal preference rather than a shared heritage. This has made community life much more difficult and contributes to a lot of conflicts.

Nevertheless, though Bishop Lohr's advice can't work as well as it once did, it will still serve a beginning pastor well. No matter how idiotic your predecessor's innovations look to you, believe me: somebody loves and treasures them, and they will see an attempt to change them as something like an attack on one of their children. Also, there will be people who may not care one way or another about styles of worship or programs but will appreciate your efforts to learn the place. You'll get a reputation for tolerance, generosity, and the ability to listen. This can open a lot of doors.

But there are two problems with this advice: one small, one great.

The small problem is that, for every person who loved the last pastor's innovations or oddities, there is another who hated them, another who couldn't wait for that pastor to leave, who perhaps worked hard to make that happen, and is now anxious to return to (or move on to) the way things ought to be. They will be standing in line to tell you this as you unpack. I didn't find this a great problem because it actually helped you know what people were thinking and, as I said, most people would understand if you told them you wanted to move slowly. An added plus was identifying the people who refused to understand so you could mark them as people to be wary of.

The greater problem with Bishop Lohr's advice is getting an accurate picture of how the congregation did things to begin with. And here's where I met one of the people who really drove me nuts.

It was at a congregation where we were doing a long-term interim. I was trying to find out how things were done during the worship service and I thought I had located the perfect person: she was a vibrant, talkative woman, very involved with the altar guild; she had a child in the confirmation program, and she and her husband had both served on the council. She was often dropping things off at the church and also ran a small business in town, so she was an easy person to contact. She looked like the perfect source.

Our first encounters went like this:

"Hey, Bev, just so I know: how do you guys do x, y, or z?"

Big smile and laugh from Bev. "Oh, wow, we're really flexible and we've done it about every way you can think of! We've done a, b, c, d—hey, sometimes we've even done p and q! Whoa! That was something! But, you know"—very serious look on Bev's face now—"we've really followed what the pastor wanted on that one. So it's whatever you want."

Trying to find out many things at the beginning, we had this conversation many times.

Then I started to notice that people kept giving me strange looks when I'd check signals with them about some event that was just about to begin.

Those encounters would go like this:

People That Drove Me Nuts (2)

Seeing the wrinkled brows, the quickly exchanged looks of puzzlement, I would say: "Um—isn't this how you guys do this?"

"Well . . . not for years. But if it's what *you* want . . . "

But that wasn't the worst of it. The worst of it was to find out Bev herself was complaining about the new ways we were doing things.

I finally realized Bev would always present you with a blizzard of options, some only a lunatic would choose; there would be one of those that was her preference, sometimes one that had nothing to do with the congregation's own preferences or history, but you would never know which one that was; she would usually leave you thinking you'd agreed about something but, if she was involved, something different would always happen and, if she wasn't involved, nothing would go right because you were attempting something new to everyone.

I started to notice, too, that she did this to everybody and, as likable as she looked, was not really as close to everyone as I had thought. I'm not sure she set out to make other people's lives difficult; in fact, I eventually gathered she believed the opposite to be true. But she seemed so pleasant and open when you first met her she was hard to spot as trouble, and she made everything a lot harder than it had to be.

People That Drove Me Nuts (3)

I ALWAYS TRIED TO make the lives of volunteers easy. We couldn't do much in the church without volunteers to teach Sunday School, maintain the building, serve on the council, do all the little things that make a church a living community rather than a one-person show one step from collapse. When I think about what was good in my years of service, I see the faces of volunteers who gave up their time and devoted their efforts with no expectation of payment or reward.

(The bad volunteers were rewarded by the power they got to push people around. The good volunteers were rewarded by grief and criticism.)

I treasured volunteers, so I tried to make their lives easy: tried to make sure they had what they needed, knew what was supposed to happen and when, weren't being asked to do the impossible. I kept meetings short and on point. I tried to be understanding and unruffled when people let me down, because I would need the same people again someday. Also, if there was a mess to be cleaned up—a bathroom accident, or a ton of dishes after a big funeral—I wanted to be one of the cleaners. I thought those things were more important than the trumpeting of "thank yous" after the dust had cleared.

If there were volunteers in the worship service, my last instruction was this: "Remember—we're not putting on a Broadway show, we're Christian disciples leading worship. It's not about perfection, but devotion." It was not only important for them to hear that; it was important for me to believe that. One of the best pieces of advice about leadership I ever found was a remark by T. E. Lawrence: it's better for the people you're leading to do something for themselves imperfectly than for you to do everything for them perfectly; also, you may find that your idea of perfection is not worth as much as you think it is. Amen, Brother Lawrence.

Now, I've gone to all this trouble to assure you I'm patient and broad-minded and tolerant and generally a wonderful person because there was one group of people for whose failings and limitations I had no patience or tolerance at all: pastors.

Nothing infuriated me more than a pastor who didn't bother to prepare, or laughed off responsibilities, or ridiculed knowledge and effort. We're the ones who are free to be prepared, paid to bear the responsibilities. There's a style of pastoral leadership I wish I could stamp out whose mission seems to be showing how silly everything in the church is. I would say this seems to be the favored style of the self-absorbed and self-satisfied but, clearly, I'm not very objective about this.

There was one encounter that summed this up for me.

I served for several years on the synod's candidacy committee, which followed seminary students from their first application letter through all their academic and fieldwork towards their ordination. This committee was the only group to see all of a candidate's records and evaluations: psychological tests, grades, intern reports. It was responsible for the final certification for ordination.

The last hurdle was this: each year, a national committee would set a final exam; it would be a linked set of essay questions (one of which, for pastoral candidates, would involve writing a sermon) probing a candidate's knowledge, experience, sense of vocation, sense of church and life, ability to respond to difficult situations. It was a lot like a grad school prelim, but with much more of a practical orientation. I can't praise the group that produced these exams highly enough: they did a tremendous job shaping provocative, revealing questions. The candidate would only have to produce about 25 or 30 pages, but the varied questions left them few places to hide. It was an academic ritual in the best sense, and it was thrilling to pore over the papers and see a personality emerge, exciting to spend a session with that personality, discussing faith and life.

I spent hours on each set, underlining, circling, cross-referencing, scribbling questions in the margin. (Once I sat on a panel with one of my old seminary professors, one of the most madly meticulous people I've ever known. I glanced at his copies: he had done the same, but with different colors of ink for different levels of significance.)

One more thing: this was a synod committee, not a local congregation's committee; no one was forced to serve on this. So we're a step up from local necessities, having to do it or it doesn't get done. This really was a task of choice.

Now to my defining encounter.

People That Drove Me Nuts (3)

Both clergy and lay members would cycle on and off this committee, and one year one of the new members was a pastor I already had reason to classify among the self-satisfied. Pastor Bob seems like a good name.

We'd usually, for final certifications, meet for a day at the synod office. We'd break into small panels, each taking one student, for sessions that lasted about an hour and a half, then meet as a committee at the end of the day.

I was on the first panel with Bob and one other member. The student entered, there were introductions, a prayer. We shifted about, we shuffled papers.

Then came the moment of sleazy, inexcusable negligence I will remember to my dying day:

Bob picked up his copy of the student's exam—it looked pristine; it looked unread, untouched; if it had been wrapped in cellophane, it couldn't have looked cleaner. He tossed it—*tossed it*—down the table, away from him, as he might toss a rat that had died of plague.

I remember being struck dumb, my mouth dropping open.

Bob leaned back in his chair, with all the satisfaction he felt about himself, and said, "Well, I don't want to get bogged down"—he nodded towards the exam—"in that."

Let's go over that again, to savor it: Bob didn't want to get "bogged down" in the papers the rest of us had been studying to prepare for this session.

I've already made clear the value I saw in these exams. But look across the table at the candidate: this young person has spent days, weeks, producing the papers Bob tossed aside, crafting thoughtful, extensive answers. That kind of work deserves serious attention from the examiners. We owe that candidate our best efforts. We respect that candidate's work—which really reflected four years of varied activity—by probing it, testing it in the best sense.

But Bob didn't want to get "bogged down"—and I thought he was going to continue: "in this bullshit." He didn't want to get bogged down by the very reason we were sitting in this room to begin with.

I don't have to tell you that Bob hadn't read any of the essays we dealt with that day. He hadn't even looked at them. He sat on this committee so he could get a day away from his parish with a good excuse and a free lunch. You noticed, of course, he nevertheless assumed he should lead the discussion.

Pastors like that drove me nuts.

People That Drove Me Nuts (4)

We were talking, during the coffee hour at some conference meeting, to a bright young woman who was also part of a clergy couple. They were newly ordained, just beginning their service. Pastors always moan to each other about their schedules, so we were going on about the meetings we had coming up. She laughed and said, "Well, there's a church council meeting tonight but we decided we never needed to go to them. I mean, it's their business what they do with the bills and the building."

It was a little like saying, "Oh, I never use silverware," or "I never wear clothes when I lead worship in the summer," or "I decided I'd never stop at stop signs. People should just watch where they're going." They are all statements about conduct that is certainly possible, just barely conceivable as a plan of action, not exactly insane, yet beyond eccentric, virtually unheard of, and—with church councils as with stop signs—not really a wise path to a long and happy future.

After a few moments of stupefied silence, we suggested that, at the very least, council meetings would be a good way to meet some fairly active congregational members as well as a way to avoid some bitter surprises.

On the other hand, not a few laypeople would agree with that young pastor. Shortly after we began serving our second parish, I made one of those harmless "seconds" to a harmless motion that passed unanimously at an uneventful council meeting. When the minutes were published, the council president got an angry phone call complaining about my doing that and claiming pastors should have no official part in council meetings. The president pointed out that, unfortunately, the constitution said we did.

But the Lutheran tradition is a blend of wildly different polities and pieties, from the nearly royalist to the radically democratic. Our first parish had its roots in the Augustana Synod: the church was understood not as "all the baptized" but as "pastors [*nota bene*] and congregations"; the pastor was the president of the church council and chaired all congregational meetings; a meeting without the pastor did not count as an official meeting. Our second parish was a product of a couple of mergers but there was a strong

People That Drove Me Nuts (4)

Norwegian Lutheran presence: the pastor was not an officer of the congregation; a lay president chaired all meetings; there was a strong feeling that pastors should have no part at all in congregational decisions.

There was a not very hidden anticlericalism among the Norwegian Lutherans which was a little hard to take, but the system itself had its advantages. Most importantly, it gave a visible presence to shared responsibility. It was good for everyone to see clearly there were other people involved in decisions besides the pastor. Also, as Bishop Lohr once told me, if you're smart enough and plan ahead, you don't have to chair the meeting to be able to run the meeting.

For me, meetings were a necessary evil. I got a reputation, which I liked, for keeping people on the subject and keeping the meetings short. I must say, however, that I didn't see council meetings as the primary locus of my leadership: I took that to be worship, especially the sermon. Thus, I was probably more comfortable than many pastors in not always having council votes go my way.

They can't and won't always go your way, especially as the old, unspoken ethnic bonds disappear and local congregations become blends of many traditions. Accepting this simple truth, like accepting the imperfections of life, is part of the path to wisdom and peace: you can't always get your way and it's pointless and destructive to fight about everything.

I could usually get a lot of what I wanted by talking to people beforehand, being patient and building support, trying to nudge them my way. I thought it was better to put off a vote than to lose a vote. But sometimes you can't do that either and, when you lose, you still have to be the pastor. You have to argue and to lose in a way that makes that possible.

(Of course, if the issues are church-defining, that's different. When the merger of churches that became the Evangelical Lutheran Church in America was taking place, there were congregations that voted themselves out of the church. Later, some congregations voted to leave the ELCA when we allowed those in committed same-sex unions to be ordained as pastors. Neither issue came to a vote in the churches we served, largely because we didn't make those things an issue. But if they had come to votes, and if I had lost those votes, I wouldn't continue as the pastor because I'd resign from the congregation. Rather, I'm writing here about the normal ups and downs of parish life.)

Some of the people that drove me nuts were the pastors I served with who could simply not accept defeat on any issue, who needed to control every aspect of the congregation's life, from the color of the kitchen cabinets to the angle of the painted lines in the parking lot.

I don't just mean they would sulk.

One of them had the strong delusion that he respected protocol and process, but what that meant for Pastor Ollie was that he could warp anything in the constitution to allow him to get his way, like the lawyers that make people hate lawyers. He boasted to us during a conference pastors' meeting that he had just called a special council meeting to reverse the decision of the women's group to spend some of their funds on kitchen improvements. He intended to appropriate that money for general church use and then to direct it to a project he had come up with that had already been voted down once by the congregation. He quoted us constitutional articles and by-laws to justify every step. We all had fun later counting up how many career-ending decisions he had managed to shape into a single act.

But it's one thing to be annoyed by these guys: it's another to get pulled into the snowballing messes they create.

We had served for so long in our first parish that we ended up being some of the longest-serving pastors in the county, of any denomination. Over time, covering for people who were on vacation, we had presided at funerals in almost all the Lutheran churches. Also, the county was so small and the people so interrelated that, since our own church averaged a funeral a month or more, we got to be pretty well known to everybody.

Getting to know a community that way is a strong bond. But, if that's the only way people know you, they probably think you're wiser and more caring than you really are. Some of them start submitting their own pastors to you for evaluation.

I hated this, but usually you could say something noncommittal or even possibly helpful, like "You should really bring this up with your own pastor." But there was one time when the phone calls began pouring in, when we couldn't walk down the street without being stopped with that chilling overture, "Say, since I ran into you, what would you do if . . . "

This wasn't a minor disagreement or clash of wills: this was behavior these people had never seen. Pastor Jack was relatively new, and he had been the one person they interviewed who fit their needs exactly, who seemed to offer everything they were looking for. (The Pastor Jacks of the church have a sixth sense for this: it's the only thing they do well.) He turned out, not surprisingly, to be the living contradiction of everything he had promised.

People That Drove Me Nuts (4)

But here's what was driving them crazy: Jack took over the writing and publishing of the council minutes. If he lost a vote or didn't get his way, he would, like the historians of the old Soviet Union, simply rewrite history and say he had.

I thought, when I first heard this, it must have been some office error. Most of the council members, the first time it happened, thought so too. But it happened often enough and I was told it often enough that we all had to admit finally that we were dealing with something truly disturbed.

I can still hear one council member on the phone, telling it and retelling it as though he still had to make himself believe it: "Pastor, I go to all the meetings. I stay for the whole meeting. Then I read the minutes and it's like they're about a different meeting."

They had approached Jack about this. He said he couldn't understand what they meant and insisted he would never do anything of the sort. Then he would do it all over again.

That was what Jack would do when he wanted something. When he didn't want to do something that enough people insisted be done, he would somehow manage to get other pastors to do it for him. You can get away with a lot when you create "shared ministries," "rotating chaplain duties," "interdenominational outreach programs." He was as good at this as he was at interviewing. At one point, I realized Jack had got the rest of us to make his hospital calls: he could see the hospital from his office; the rest of us had to make special trips.

The worst part was always being on the spot when people wanted to know what you thought about their pastor. I think, towards the end of his service, I was reduced to saying something like: "I honestly don't know what you should do about your pastor." If I knew the person well, I might add, "He drives me nuts, too."

But what can really drive you nuts is when someone like this not only acts underhandedly to do something no one else wants done but also manages to blame you for it.

One of the bishops we served under became bishop through no fault of his own. The candidate who should have been bishop got caught in the conservative backlash (anti-ecumenical, antigay, anti-you name it) that was warping so much of what we did at the time. The candidate the conservatives recruited to run was so poorly qualified he lost votes every time he spoke. So, in desperation, they threw their support behind a rather belligerent, obsessive person who shouldn't even have been on the shortlist. (He won, but his supporters lived to regret it.)

He wasn't a terrible bishop but he was obsessive: when he wanted something, he was like a dog chasing a rabbit. Let's call him Bishop Iago.

He decided he wanted to get rid of someone on the synod staff, someone much more well known and much more popular than he was. Let's call him Cassio.

In fairness to Iago, other bishops had wanted to get rid of Cassio as well, but found, to their regret, it wasn't easy to do.

So here's what Iago did: he met with the synod executive council, discussed budget constraints and staff needs, and had them formally agree that a communications director was needed on the staff. Cassio's name was never mentioned.

Iago then informed Cassio that the executive council had voted to terminate his position because they needed to fund a communications director. That they had never mentioned Cassio's name or had any idea their decision bore on his position was not mentioned. As far as Cassio knew, Iago had nothing to do with this.

Cassio was not a shy person, nor one to suffer in silence. His supporters quickly found out he was terminated.

I happened to know a couple members of the executive council. The first they knew of this mess was the morning after Cassio spread his news, when they received one furious, abusive phone call after another.

They denied, truthfully, even discussing Cassio's position. Cassio insisted, truthfully, he was out of a job. All these people being trusted more than the bishop, it wasn't hard to piece together the full story. Bishop Iago served out his term, but he was finished as the bishop.

The Bishop Iagos and Pastor Jacks always imagine they're more skilled, more clever, more successful in manipulation than they are. Blinded by their desires, by their need to get their way, they're blind to how nakedly deceitful they finally appear to those they've undercut. They think they can shift blame forever, when once is enough to destroy their moral force as leader.

You start recognizing the type after a while, but they never stop driving you nuts.

People That Drove Me Nuts (5)

If you spend very much time around Lutherans, you've heard some version of the following jokes:

Q: How many Lutherans does it take to change a light bulb?
A: Change? We'd rather sit in the dark any day.
Q: What are the seven last words of the church?
A: We never did it that way before.

If you're a Lutheran, you've been in some congregation that was ridiculed, often by its own pastor, for being unexciting, uptight, unadventurous, fossilized, frozen in its ways, and incapable of change.

I served with a few of these Prophets of Change. I got very tired of being subjected to their pronouncements.

But, one day at a conference gathering, I was listening to one of them whom I knew, and I had a revelation. He himself never changed. He introduced one change after another in every congregation he served but he was making them adjust to him: new styles of worship, new sound systems, new arrangements of the chancel and nave, new times for worship, new schedules for meetings. New to them, not to him: he uprooted their habits so he could continue in his own. He preached change, but what he meant was everyone else should change so he could be comfortable.

Comfortable and in control: if you constantly spring new things and new arrangements on people, you'll be the only one who knows what's going on. Congregations will be reduced to audiences watching a performance.

I also found, for all the preaching of novelty that went on, the innovations brought by these prophets were often not very novel at all. The innovations usually came down to *not* doing some traditional Lutheran practice. I was stunned once to attend a service led by a pastor who was plugging an alternative hymnal: he used none of its liturgies and picked hymns from it that Charles Wesley and Robert Lowry would have felt at home singing. His worship service had about as much novelty as an early-nineteenth-century camp meeting.

People That Drove Me Nuts (5)

Things like this, for the most part, remain at the level of the silly and the merely annoying. But I think they can lead us to something a bit more important.

In all the situations I've alluded to, the prophets of change get all the attention, but I'd like to point out something I consider more important: how tolerant the Lutheran congregations are that put up with them.

Communities sometimes do overlook, and even lament, their best qualities, so it's worthwhile to point them out from time to time. All those qualities Lutherans are ridiculed for can be described much more positively: let's start with tolerant and add moderate, thoughtful, cautious, quiet, self-critical, respectful of the past.

Anyone who looks at the religions of the world today, the fanatics who derail all compromises, the ignorant loudmouths that fill the airwaves, the murderous killers, the screaming fundamentalists of every faith, anyone who seriously contemplates this ghastly religious landscape and thinks it's a *flaw*—a flaw deserving of relentless mockery—to be tolerant, moderate, thoughtful, and quiet, is a blind fool.

It might be noticed, too, that the branch of the Lutheran family I served in, the Evangelical Lutheran Church in America, these fossilized, unchanging Lutherans, voted at their National Assembly to recognize committed same-sex unions and to ordain as pastors those who are in such committed relationships. These Lutherans proved themselves more welcoming of change than most of their fellow believers, as well as their fellow citizens.

It would not be irrelevant to add, while discussing Lutheran character, that the forces opposed to the Assembly actions consistently underestimated the strength and the resolve of these quiet, tolerant people.

The Church Heals the Help

We attended, on internship, one of the most disciplined Bible study groups I've ever seen outside of a classroom. The conference pastors would meet Thursday morning and one of them would present a paper—typed, distributed—on the texts for the Sunday after the next. Thus, when you began preparing the next week, you already had a rough-and-ready commentary that you had spent an hour or so debating with some pretty bright people. Some of them carried in their Greek New Testaments, and they regularly referred to its text.

One day, as the session wound down, the conversation turned to scheduling, arranging time, not having enough time. There was a kind of elder statesman in the group, a large, jovial man who always wore three-piece suits, and liked to project an aura of earthy wisdom. He leaned back in his chair, shook his head, and said, "I've never understood that complaint. I get up around five o'clock, do my theological reading and sermon study before nine, then I'm in the office until noon. In the afternoon, I make hospital calls, visit shut-ins, keep up with the home communions, contact the people I need to. In the evening, I have meetings, classes, counseling sessions, and"—he shrugged—"if I don't, then I can make a few more visits when people are home from work."

No one really said very much after that, and we all drifted away to our separate cars. Before I go on, let me ask this, class:

Did you keep up with the math? Hmmm, let's see: start with 3 hours, well, say 4 to be generous, another 3, then probably about 4 or so because visiting isn't as controllable as office work, umm, carry the 1, then we've got, say, 3 more to be on the safe side. That about it?

I get something like a 14-hour work day. It goes about five in the morning to ten at night for 17 hours, minus 3 for food, washing, and other necessities. We assume either no family or a wife and children that get none of his time. Is that what you got? Say he takes one afternoon and one day off for an 80-hour week.

The Church Heals the Help

I was adding up the hours in my head as he was talking and I remembered delightedly that I had once actually worked 80 hours a week. I worked in an oil refinery that scheduled double shifts when a unit was shut down for major cleaning and maintenance. You're OK the first week, the second week you're trying to work in a nap when things are quiet, the third week you're hoping you can stay awake because you're working close to some pretty unforgiving machinery, you're making stupid mistakes and getting clumsy, the fourth week you may be there but you're no longer working those 80 hours. The days you're off don't feel like days off: you sleep late and you're groggy, then you're back at the plant. If this goes on too long, you'll be lucky not to get hurt.

You do that when there are things that need to be done and you can't afford to waste time. You don't do that as your normal schedule if you expect to have a long and healthy career of service. Where I worked, it was an occasional necessity. When low-paid workers are forced to work that schedule regularly, it's exploitation and virtual slavery, and you can bet they're getting hurt. Certainly, pastors, like every committed professional, will end up working some 80-hour weeks. But when it's seriously put forward as the normal schedule for someone who needs to be alert, thoughtful, sensitive, and effective, it's nothing but bullshit and doesn't deserve to be taken seriously.

I also once had the opportunity to meet—and more importantly, observe—another pastor who claimed to work an 80-hour week. We had a job as janitors in a big urban church, and the head pastor liked to roam the church and chat a bit as he passed by. He had a while to go to be retired (and the ministry was a second career for him), but he was already looking forward to it. This is what he said about his schedule: "It would really be nice when I retire to serve as a chaplain somewhere—a hospital or a nursing home. Work about a 40-hour week. You know"—he looked down on me as I was scrubbing a spot on the floor and smiled—"about half-time." Class? Calculate thus: $40=1/2$, therefore, $80=1$ (i.e., full time).

Since he didn't tell me when he woke up, let's use some different numbers. So: he may have arrived at nine in the morning and gone home at nine at night: that's 12, if you're generous in the count and include meals as work; eliminating all days off, then OK, you can get 84 hours a week, call it even for being generous with meal times. Again, no family life included.

People who never do janitorial work, maintenance work, lawn work, who never clean toilets or collect garbage, don't realize how much the

All Hands Stand By to Repel Boarders

people who do that work see and hear. I'll put it this way: whatever this guy thought he did for 80 hours every week, it wasn't something I would call work.

So my own varied work history had well equipped me to take the measure of that speech. By the time we reached the parking lot, I had dismissed it with all the other fantastic bilge I'd already heard from seminary professors, and I was ready for lunch.

Gary, my supervisor, was driving that day. I already thought he was a good pastor—devoted, intense, a powerful preacher, a gifted counselor with time for everyone, a serious scholar. (The year I was with him, he was using the Latin New Testament for exegesis, to get a different slant on the texts.) Looking back now, I would say he and my friend Ken were the two best I ever served with. No contest, no qualification.

Gary turned to me before he started the car. He looked pretty mad. He said, "Listen to me. Don't take anything in that speech you just heard seriously. I don't know why he thinks he can say that stuff in front of young pastors. It's ridiculous. Nobody can live like that. If he does now, he didn't always, and I can't believe he does now. Try to do that and you'll kill yourself. You'll die alone, too, because your wife will be long gone."

Well, I thought, that settles that.

On that drive back, as well as other times during the year, Gary talked a lot about managing time, working efficiently, controlling your time, guarding your family time rigidly, drawing limits.

He was a driven guy, and I think he had to be intensely conscious of the limits he thought should be set or he would find the work consuming him. I think he reacted so angrily that morning because, while he would never give that speech, he was all too likely to find himself living it, without realizing it.

Any devoted pastor might: there are things you must prepare alone, there are volunteers you must work with when their jobs allow them to be free, there are unforeseeable demands that respect no one's time—illnesses, accidents, deaths, troubled people. All of these fill the hours and, when the hours are full, more demands arrive.

Gary was always sensitive to the need to be available for troubled people, unforeseen demands. So he had rough goals for his time and his regular tasks, but nothing rigid. He had me keep a visiting log: he said to aim at five to ten serious encounters a week (hospital visits, home visits, talks with parents), then evaluate: if you found you were doing less or more, look for the reason. He thought meetings, counseling sessions, classes, inevitably took your nights, but you had to control them: if you were tied up for more than three nights every week, look for the reason and make a change: group the meetings, make them short and, if nothing else, start saying no or take time off during the day. (This came back to me forcefully the first year I served: I realized I had spent twenty-one straight nights at either meetings, visits, and classes, or involved in some necessary preparation I didn't get time for during the day. All pastors will understand when I say: I was so exhausted I felt virtuous; I thought it would be heroic to keep it up. I heard Gary scolding me in my head, and I started saying no.)

I think it's wrong and destructive for pastors—and, worse, congregations and councils—to obsess over hours, rigid schedules, time logs. Pastors are not office staff, but pastoral staff. They don't have an hourly job, but a calling, a mission. Most of them, in the typical small parish, are on call around the clock.

Incompetent or lazy pastors can't be made to work hard. Good, devoted pastors don't need to be told to work hard: they need to be told to set limits. Another thing Gary liked to point out was that only you know how many commitments you've already made, how many times you've gone to the hospital, how much the last death and funeral took out of you: people have a right to ask for your time, but you have a right to say no. And you have the duty to keep yourself alert, thoughtful, sensitive, and effective.

By the time I was nearing the end of my service, it had begun to dawn even on the church hierarchy that the health of pastors was becoming a serious issue. The conference pastors' meetings I attended seemed to deal with stress more often than theology and biblical interpretation. When the local pastor chose the program, some variation of "what's killing me and not letting me sleep" was a distressingly frequent topic.

We had lots of seminars about staying healthy. Over and over again, I heard speakers note: ministers were once the most healthy group in America and were now the least. We got help with our medical costs if we would complete wellness programs. I got handed more copies than I wanted of something I think was called the wholeness or wellness wheel: a color-coded wheel of six aspects of well-being (social, physical, emotional, etc.). It was a classic problem-solving tool: breaking down a large, vague problem into smaller, definable problems, clarifying attention and direction. It wasn't so bad as a simple tool to hand somebody, but the most important thing about all this was to make people feel able to act, to stop being helpless corks in the floodwaters overwhelming them. In fact, we were once again not far from the therapies of ancient philosophy, the Stoics and the Epicureans: the careful weighing of life's forces and limits, how to find power, how to avoid wounding, when to yield, what to cling to.

One of the most powerful and provocative things I've ever read about trauma and healing is the Regeneration Trilogy by the British novelist Pat Barker, about the treatment of shell-shocked soldiers in World War I. There was one observation in it that surprised me and that I think is relevant here. It was easy to think that the traumas of the young infantry officers were caused by the horrible conditions of trench warfare: the filth, the mud, the relentless bombardments, the mutilations and deaths happening right next to them. Indeed, shell shock implies a definite cause. Then one of the doctors noticed he was seeing the same conditions in men who were in observation balloons: above the filth, the mud, not being shelled, yet in a sense sitting ducks, extremely vulnerable to attack by fighter planes with no way to fight back. His conclusion was that it wasn't the dirt or the shells that traumatized the soldiers, but their acute sense of powerlessness, helpless vulnerability, suffered for too long.

This example shows, of course, in an extreme way, that there is some suffering that can't be escaped or acted against.

But not all troubles are that extreme, and troubles need not be extreme to harm you. It's good to be summoned to take action and to be shown a direction.

And much of it turns on the lessons Gary gave me at the start of my service: attend to time, don't lose control of it; protect your time, don't let anyone else define it for you; define it for your whole life, what you value, who you are.

I want to close this section with one observation.

I think to focus much of this advice one thing has to be made explicit: apart from attending to the various factors of life and health, there's a center to the pastoral calling itself and you have to find it and be faithful to it. If you know you're there to preach, teach, and lead the community in its worship, everything else you do will fall into place. You act from those central tasks. Knowing what you're doing and why you're doing it will be a source of strength at the very center of your life.

That focus itself, of course, can bring you trouble and criticism: people understand any amount of visible activity, however pointless, more than they understand sitting alone in silence, shaping the challenge of the gospel into a sermon. Pastors probably get more applause for taking youth groups to amusement parks than they do for spending serious time on their sermons. But, unless we wanted to be tour guides and entertainers to begin with, I can't make myself believe that's where our strength lies.

Four Statements You Should Know How to Make

1/ That was my fault.

2/ I don't know.

3/ I'm sorry.

4/ No.

PART FOUR

Of Little Faith (2)

Shortly after we arrived at the second parish we would serve, the local Assembly of God church began talking about a youth church they wanted to develop. It would gather all the young people from all the churches, hold its own Sunday services and other activities, and be led by the current Assembly youth leader.

They talked it up among the town's parents, using that magic phrase: they wanted to "do something for the youth." Unlike, presumably, the "nothing" everyone else was doing.

I thought this was a dreadful idea, but the worst thing about it was that it was happening so soon after our arrival, before I knew much about the town and its churches and before I had a chance to build any relationships with people I would need as allies. The woman who led the youth group at our church was a generous, tolerant person who saw no reason to distrust people who called themselves Christians.

By this time in my service, fairly or not, I had a pretty negative view of the Assembly of God and its leaders. I found they would never cooperate in a program or activity unless they ran it. I thought they liked to frighten kids with apocalyptic scenarios and tended to preach a punitive, self-righteous brand of Christianity. They were rabid critics of public education, especially science and literature classes, and any instruction that touched on sex. I found them dismally ignorant of Christianity itself and its various branches. I thought they were part of what was poisoning American life.

I would have trouble letting leaders from the Assembly of God give my dog a dog biscuit, let alone support their exclusive oversight of the spiritual lives of the community's children.

But the very idea of a youth church is a terrible idea. One of the best things about a congregation is that it spans so many generations. Especially in the small churches we served, kids got to know not only the other kids' parents, but also the faithful adults who taught Sunday School; they interacted with the elderly members, who loved having them around. They got used to being in a larger community beyond their family and school;

they learned how to be part of something like that. The older people got to see who would care for the things they cared for. You could see the different generations being blessings to each other. Even apart from church life, serious studies of healthy communities usually show young people benefit from more, not less, interaction with adults. I think the only adult that was going to be involved in this youth church was the Assembly youth leader, whom I thought of as a big kid in an adult body. This would be like having high school without any teachers, ceding control to the loudest and most domineering kids.

But you could get away with a lot in those small towns if you called yourself a Christian and said you were going to do something for young people.

I did a lot of talking in the weeks after I heard about this. The Methodist pastor was as horrified as I was. The local Roman Catholic priest was absolutely amazed that anyone would think he would support his young people regularly attending some other church.

When our local ministerial group met and this idea was formally presented to us, I think the people from the Assembly were stunned that anyone would object to what they wanted to do. They really do see themselves as the pure Christian strain: when we differ from them, they see us as at best wrong, at worst devious, malicious cultural sell-outs with hidden agendas. I don't know that we convinced them about the variety of Christian belief and practice, but it was clear they would get no support from us.

Here's my favorite moment from that meeting:

They kept protesting what an innocent idea they had, how pure their intentions were; they kept invoking their magic phrase—"do something for young people," the phrase so powerful with parents worried about their teenagers, so powerless with pastors who didn't trust them. But they made the mistake of putting that point negatively, as an accusation: that the other churches, our churches, were doing nothing for young people.

We let it pass once. The second time it was said, the Roman Catholic priest, whom I had never heard speak in anger, let alone raise his voice, suddenly turned red, raised his fist over his head and smashed it down on the table, making coffee cups leap and eyeballs pop. He bellowed, "Stop saying my church does nothing for its young people! Stop it!"

It was one of those moments that end a discussion, no matter how long anyone keeps talking.

Now here's my suggestion:

Of Little Faith (2)

Let's all imagine ourselves sitting in front of that furious priest. Let's take that advice he bellowed. Let's stop saying our church does nothing for its young people.

You could hear that spoken almost everywhere I served, about almost every church. If you're going to quit a church and want a reason no one will question, say it doesn't do enough for young people and everyone will nod. If you don't like the pastor and need a criticism no one will argue with, say he or she hasn't done enough for young people and everyone will nod.

When this charge isn't simply an irrational attack, what it usually means is that there are no visible programs explicitly targeting people of high school age, or not enough of them. I think it's wonderful if concerned adults want to work with young people on service projects and group activities. But I see no point in getting hysterical about them. I certainly don't assume that young people who aren't involved in them have no faith, or that churches that can't get them started or get much of a turnout are failing.

I think the real problem is we can't see what's right in front of us and we have no faith in what we're doing. Neither churches nor parents want to let teenagers out of their sight. We have no faith in what we've given them.

The young people in every church I served were given years of instruction in Sunday School and Vacation Bible School. We never supported sending them out of the service but always welcomed them there: many of them could recite the creed, the Lord's prayer, and other prayers by heart without realizing they had learned them; they heard the gospel discussed, probed, and proclaimed Sunday after Sunday for years. When they were in junior high, we had them in confirmation class. We did both two-year and three-year programs, built on Luther's catechism: a half year each on the ten commandments, the creed, the Lord's prayer, the sacraments. Moral issues were discussed through all the lessons. The students took turns leading the opening prayer services. In other words, once a week, for at least two years, within a devotional context, the young people of the church would sit down in a small group with a pastor and talk about, ask about, think about, laugh about, learn about, and struggle with the life of faith. They did service projects and some of them were regular worship leaders.

All this would be normal in the Lutheran church. We'll forget about camping and skiing trips.

I think it's stupid to describe that as "doing nothing for young people."

Role Models

Early on, in applying to seminary, we had to take what seemed like an endless series of tests probing our personalities in various ways. One, I recall, was to test our sense of vocation and asked us about people we looked up to and admired. At the time, I listed people like Thomas Merton and Daniel Berrigan, whom I did (and still do) admire. Most of us, obviously, would also list teachers and, since many of my teachers had been nuns, priests, or Methodist pastors, I came across as fairly focused in my vocation as a pastor.

Later on, when you're trying to change calls or be considered for a new call, you have to fill out the same kinds of profiles. By then, I was thinking a little more concretely, and I realized that my earliest and most powerful role models came from the school of Hollywood, the old movies I watched passionately on television: those paeans to courage, loyalty, righteous battle, costly idealism, and selfless sacrifice. Instead of Berrigan and Merton, I should have said I wanted to be like Errol Flynn and John Wayne: not the self-indulgent drunk or the swaggering, right-wing poseur, but the fearless idealists of the movies who walked out of the television screen into my heart.

John Wayne came to be a joke, a symbol of everything that was wrong with a bloated, belligerent superpower, but anyone who grew up when I did and knew Wayne from his great movies with John Ford would have seen something else. I've begun telling people, when this subject comes up, that any man my age who doesn't list John Wayne as a role model is either deluding himself or lying.

One of my moral touchstones still is the officer Wayne plays in Ford's *Fort Apache*: competent, gentle, funny, compassionate, concerned about the troops he leads, concerned about the Native Americans he thinks are being abused. He does everything he can to stop a war, even standing up publicly to his commander. Then, when everything goes to pieces, he's the one who rebuilds his shattered and morally compromised regiment, having to swallow a lot of garbage in the process so he can do that.

When I rewatched the movie as an adult, I effortlessly recalled my small self, staring up at the screen, wanting to grow up to be like that guy.

Idolizing someone who was trying to be effective and maintain his integrity in a compromised and compromising organization was probably not so bad a preparation for serving in the church.

Occupational Hazards (2): the Perils of Decency

WE OFTEN DID FUNERALS for people in the area who were only distantly connected to the church. Especially when we served on the Canadian border, a decent burial still meant one that involved a service in a church building.

It meant that because the church—like the school, the city hall, and the sheriff's office—was one of the visible pillars of decent society in that place. This was something more primitive than respect, something connected to clearing fields and killing wolves. We were part of the way order was kept. Prophetic or even mildly liberal pastors might not like that, but they weren't going to change it.

One Sunday morning, a very pleasant young woman I'd never met approached me in the narthex before the service. She told me her name, then looked away and said, "I guess I know what you think of my life, but I'd like to talk to you about doing my mom's funeral."

I was so stunned by her first comment I didn't have a comeback. Thinking about it today, I wish I'd said something like: "You probably have no idea how much you just insulted me." Being fairly sarcastic, I was at first tempted to say, "Honestly, I never think about you at all," but she had mentioned a funeral, which commands respect, and my surprise gave me a little time to think so what I came up with was: "Um—we've never met and I really don't know anything about you, so why don't we start from there?"

I tried to sound as neutral as I could. I wished she hadn't come at me as she did, but I know why she did: if she hadn't, she would still be assuming I was judging her every moment we talked. She wanted to make a preemptive strike, like people who ridicule their own clumsiness or fatness: they grant you the judgment and hope you can move on.

There was no question in her mind that I would have a low opinion of her. She concluded this not because she knew anything about me—or very much about Jesus for that matter—but because she thought she had a clear idea of what the church stood for.

By then, I would have known I couldn't tell her she was wrong. I didn't have to judge her or think about her. Other Christians, past and present, local and national, had done it for me.

There can't have been many pastors of my age who went through seminary without wanting to speak for the prophetic side of the church. One of the great Christian realities of the time was Martin Luther King's civil rights crusade, the undeniable appearance among us of a New Exodus for American Christians, black and white. We also had before us, negatively, growing up in the shadow of World War II, the corruption of the German church under the Nazi party, corruption very much bound to decency, wholesomeness, purity. Lutherans might convince themselves that Dietrich Bonhoeffer was the sign of what we should be.

But any prophetic instincts you might have, any yearnings for the romance of the outsider and the outlaw, were undercut constantly by the logic of your position as an officer of an institution, an institution seen by everyone around you as a pillar of decent society.

We knew some people for years before we found out they had adult children, living in the same town, children they never mentioned to us because they were ashamed of the lives they had chosen. We were approached by families we'd known for years to do funerals for elderly black sheep they never spoke of: when we agreed, we were treated as though we had performed a miracle of generosity.

But it's not only other people that force this upon you.

George Orwell wrote a famous essay on Kipling that often came back to me during my years of service. Kipling, he said, was an unusual and valuable writer because he put himself inside the lives of people in power, people who have to make daily, unending decisions, who can't avoid responsibility because they're stuck with it. Outsiders, critics, those out of power, never really have to answer the question: In such and such circumstances, what would you *do*? People in charge, people with responsibility, people on duty, can't avoid that question, and they have to live with their answers.

It's a life-changing experience to be sitting in a meeting discussing some miserable dilemma with no good solutions and to have everyone go silent and look at you, and you realize your name is going to be on the decision.

Occupational Hazards (2): the Perils of Decency

You discover sympathy for leaders. You become a little slower to criticize them; you become a lot slower to criticize colleagues. When you hear a complaint about one of them, you assume you're never—*never*—getting the whole story.

You know how murky problems can be. You know how catastrophically things can go wrong. You know, too well, how rare good options can be. You would always love to hear angry critics be asked: "OK—so what would *you* have done?"

When I hear of any profession attacked for having a "code of silence," I know that, whatever the merits of the attack, there's something deeper at work that will never go away: the insider's knowledge of how hard decisions are, how uncontrollable circumstances and consequences are, how fantastically distorted the reports of angry and hurt people can be. You don't need an explicit code to want to keep your mouth shut about some things.

You know how dumb you can be, how tired, how distracted, how rushed, how blind. You know how lucky you've been when things that should have gone wrong didn't. You know there are things you'll regret forever.

Because, no doubt, of my growing sympathy with people stuck with representing established order, I became interested at one time in the life of Cotton Mather, one of the more famous punching bags of American religious history.

Mather was probably the greatest mind in the seventeenth-century American colonies. He had the curiosity and the civic spirit of those later American Enlightenment heroes Benjamin Franklin and Thomas Jefferson. He was a Fellow of the Royal Society with a great interest in science and a vast intellectual correspondence. He didn't believe much more religious nonsense than Isaac Newton did.

But what he's remembered for is his involvement with the Salem witch trials, the deadly nonsense of religious hysteria that killed innocent people. His reputation is such that people might be forgiven for thinking he drove the hysteria and led the persecution.

Mather certainly believed in witches and saw the devil at work around him. But he neither drove nor led the persecution and was far from bloodthirsty. What he did, however, made him infamous: he defended the trials and the killings without qualification. You can still get his account, *The Wonders of the Invisible World*, in a cheap paperback, a longtime bestseller, and examine the evidence for witchcraft in all its horrifying hollowness and obvious malice.

The irony in this is that the evidence he presents might have been evidence he himself would not have accepted. Nor would he have set loose the wild, snowballing accusations that marked those events. But Mather made a deliberate decision to defend the judges, the trials, the entire twisted horror story, because he feared people would turn against the state and its officers for perpetrating the killing. Silence would have been more forgivable. He defended the indefensible to protect the powerful.

In other words, he had once heard the devil's offer of worldly power that Jesus heard in the wilderness and, unlike Jesus, he took the deal. He thought the fate of the Christian church was so closely bound to the fate of the government, in all its works, that he felt he had to defend whatever cruelty that government handed out at all costs.

Mather wasn't the first or the last Christian leader to sink willingly into the embrace of earthly power. The same embrace has been corrupting the Roman Catholic church for centuries. It's corrupting American Christians: in the last years of my service, Christian voices supported the assassination and the torture of America's enemies; Christians feared contamination by gays and lesbians as much as the people of Salem feared contamination by witches, and did everything they could to exclude them from society.

But those are extreme cases of the hazard all Christian leaders face as soon as we are installed as leaders of such a successful, respected community, a pillar of society in the best, as well as the worst, sense. (The longer I served, the more often I reminded everyone, including myself, that it was people like us that killed Jesus.)

Let me add one more twist.

I was standing in the narthex another Sunday morning when I saw another young person walking across the lawn toward the front door. He didn't look like a typical churchgoer. He was thin and tall, with a long stride, and he was dressed in black jeans and a black T-shirt. He looked intense, intimidating. He had long, dark hair and a thick mustache, with dark stubble. I thought he must be a transient looking for some help or somebody whose car had broken down.

Then it dawned on me that I knew this kid. His name was Patrick and he was the son of a couple of our regular members. This time I did know a little bit about the life approaching me: I knew it had had its ups and downs,

Occupational Hazards (2): the Perils of Decency

but nothing that would make me not welcome him. However, I confess I still thought he was after anything but what he had really come for.

It was pretty crowded in the narthex, so I couldn't get to Patrick when he opened the door. Instead, I got to see the reactions of everyone else. The crowd parted before him like the Red Sea before the children of Israel, backs turning to him slightly, eyes glancing sideways, brows creasing, mouths turning down. The open door to the nave was only about eight feet from the front door. Patrick made a parade-ground turn and headed right for it.

We had then, as a theoretically welcoming modern church, two "greeters" assigned for each Sunday. Their task was to greet everyone arriving, welcome visitors and have them sign the guest book, and generally be available with bright smiles and information. Ours usually stood shoulder to shoulder, right next to the ushers, right at the door of the nave, like sheep in a storm. Instead of helpful greeters, we presented a kind of gauntlet of handshakes as the price of entry.

As Patrick took a step toward the nave, the first greeter, a tiny, pleasant woman, stepped in front of him, blocking his way. She pointed her finger up at his chest and said, very sternly, "What do *you* want?"

I was beginning to enjoy this. Patrick had dealt with his share of challenges from authority figures so he was unfazed and said, "I wanted to go to church."

The greeter's mouth tightened. She said, "Oh."

She looked him slowly up and down, then stepped out of his path, jerked her head toward the nave and said, "Get in." She made me think of a drill sergeant reluctantly and disgustedly dismissing a recruit.

Patrick walked in confidently and, instead of slinking into one of the rear pews, marched to the very first pew on the pulpit side, the pew no one sits in unless forced to. Every head in the church followed his progress.

Every eye in the church was on him during the service. He was the first person ushered out and you might have thought the king was leaving, as heads turned with his movement. He shook our hands, nodded and walked out the front door without speaking to anyone. After the service, we wondered, as pastors do, if we'd see him again and why on earth he had come in the first place.

That week at confirmation, the kids couldn't wait to ask me about him: "Who was that guy on Sunday? You know, the *big* guy—the dude that was all in black—who was he?" It was probably the most exciting thing they'd seen happen in church.

So I told them whose son he was, pointed out that he had sat where they were sitting not that long ago, and generally tried to temper their astonishment that a young adult male, raised in the church, might drop in on the occasional worship service. Not that I didn't think it was as weird as they did.

I had been chuckling through the week about my tiny greeter barring the way of this tall, dark intruder. I only learned later about our further efforts to drive Patrick away.

Our financial secretary, Gladys, who collected the offering money after church, was an observant and obsessive person. She had done the job so long and was so aware of the sitting patterns of the regulars that she could tell by the layering of the money in the plates who had given how much. I sometimes wondered why we bothered with envelopes.

Since Patrick sat in the first pew, his offering would have been easy to spot in any case: on the very bottom of the pulpit-side plate lay what Gladys would only describe as a "huge wad" of money.

To her credit, Gladys is the one who told me, rather ruefully, what she did next. When she brought me the story, I stopped her at this point and asked, "So how much?"

She gave me a steady look, nodded her head slowly, and said, "A lot. I mean: *a lot*."

So much, in fact, judged from the perspective of a sane churchgoer, that Gladys decided—on that evidence alone—that Patrick must have been drunk, fumbled in his jeans for the one dollar bill he should have given, unwittingly pulled out every cent he had and dropped it in the plate.

Gladys decided to do what any decent Christian would have done: she got in her car and drove around town, looking for Patrick *so she could give his money back.*

Here's another thing I learned: Gladys knew where to look. Patrick was a friend of the son of hers I had not known she had. She knocked on his door, asked for Patrick, and pushed the money at him, saying, "Here. I know you didn't mean to give this."

She was standing close enough to him now to know he hadn't been drinking. Her confidence in her interpretation of events began to erode. Patrick held up his hands and said, "No, I did mean to give it."

She pushed again. "You know there's a lot there . . . "

Patrick said—and I imagine him speaking as though to a child, "Can't the church use it? Isn't the church a good place to give your money to?"

Occupational Hazards (2): the Perils of Decency

When she told me what he said, it seemed less like a rhetorical question than a challenge, a reminder of something we might forget. I also had more reason to wonder if we'd ever see Patrick again, now that we had tried to give his money back.

But we did. From that Sunday until we left the parish, Patrick came to every worship service, sat alone in the front pew, spoke little and gave much.

I used to tell this story at evangelism seminars and at workshops about becoming a welcoming church. We did everything to push this young man away short of having the ushers drag him out. Not only did the greeters not welcome him, they actively blocked his entrance. The financial secretary tried to make him take his offering back. Then he became one of the most regular and most supportive members we had.

Now, I don't object to welcoming strategies like having greeters or having the restrooms clearly marked. It's really nice to know where the restrooms are. But holding such things up as the marks of a welcoming church, let alone part of the gathering power of the church itself, seems to me at worst a delusion and at best much ado about not much. (Remember: it was the *greeter* that tried to keep Patrick out.) Our intoxication with our own strategies is another way we display our little faith.

I guessed later what had brought Patrick to us. Something had changed in his life. An illness had come to someone he loved and he wanted to move toward that person with everything in him. Part of that move was to enter, or reenter, the community of faith he had grown up in.

If you can find any faith, you might want to see the Spirit moving in those events.

But this is why I'm telling this story here: it was our being part of decent society that made us try to push Patrick away. *But it was our being part of decent society that made Patrick come to us.*

It made me think of Groucho Marx's mind-twisting wisecrack: that he wouldn't belong to a club that would accept someone like him as a member.

Maybe I should say: this gave me something I'm not sure how to think about. I suppose I'd like to say that I was again missing what was right in front of me: that our comical efforts to exclude someone didn't amount to much and that we eventually embraced, even bragged about, Patrick's presence. But, given that Patrick always was one of us and that everyone eventually realized who he was, that doesn't seem like much of a victory. If

145

it was anyone's victory, it was Patrick's. Or, as I said, you might try thinking about the work of the Spirit.

But I'm not sure how this story bears on the church and its embrace of decent society and the exclusions of earthly power and pride.

I was tempted to end by saying: I have no idea what Jesus would think about this either. But I do have one idea: I think Jesus would probably say we spend too much time wondering how good we are—one way or another.

Try to stop that.

The Iceberg

We once had a special congregational meeting that had been poisoned beforehand by some unusually twisted rumors. People had come to be angry. The pews were so packed you might have thought we were handing out free lottery tickets.

Our council president was the high school football coach, as well as the head of the teachers' union, an affable, calm, patient man that everybody liked, and he did his best to separate truth from fiction and to lead a rational discussion. But people had come to be angry, and some of them didn't want to be anything else. Finally, another council member, Gene, a burly deputy sheriff with a bit of a temper himself, rose up in volcanic disgust and bellowed, "Any of you people think you can do a better job, you can have my council seat. Just come to the next meeting and I'll go home." He glared at the room as though he were looking at a jail cell full of drug-dealing child molesters, then sat down slowly, managing to make his stillness seem like a threat. At least this gave us a moment of silence.

I looked at John, the president. He was also still, looking heavenward. I could see Rick, our last council president, staring at the floor and shaking his head.

Well, we got the vote we needed but it was a bitter victory. What you want is for people to come to you and say, "Pastor! We were such fools to listen to the people that started the rumors! I mean, we know they're abusive morons! We don't even like them much! Why did we believe them?!?!" Failing that, you walk around for days with your stomach in knots, arguing with all the people grumbling in your head.

Somebody did come to me after that meeting, though: the deputy sheriff. He said he felt terrible about losing his temper and needed to apologize. He wasn't the only angry person at the meeting, or the nastiest. But apparently he was the only one who regretted it.

That meeting really bothered me. We had a newsletter coming out and, since it was all I could think about anyway, I thought I should write something up about what happened, about how we ought to live together as Christians. I couldn't do it. Every time I looked at that piece of paper and thought about the rumors and the anger, I started to rage myself. The more I tried, the more words I rejected, the more furious I got. So I did what I always do when I'm stuck: I wrote that I was stuck and why: I said I tried to write about the meeting but found that I just kept getting angry.

Then I said: so I decided I had to let someone else talk. I would listen with everyone else. I quoted a passage from the Epistle of James about the tongue being a fire in need of taming. Then I quoted a prayer for the healing of divisions, again written by someone else. That was it.

I thought this was a clever way to get out of my impasse while still bringing a needful word. Anyway, I felt better.

I didn't hear any comments on this. I assumed people just shrugged it off as more pastor babble. I certainly didn't think it could make anybody furious.

Then one day I was alone in the office, and John peeked around the door. He always got right to the point. "Hey. Got a call from—" Hmm. What name shall I use for this lady, such a rancid and relentless complainer and rumormonger? Ah, I have it: we'll call her Mendacia.

"Hey. Got a call from Mendacia. She didn't like what you wrote."

"Um—"

He held up his hand. "And—she thinks I should bring it up at council and have the council formally censure you or something. At least yell at you in loud voices."

I think I laughed, not in merriment but astonishment. "Really? For—quoting the Bible and . . . praying?"

"Well, I think it was the particular quote you picked."

"Still . . ."

"Anyway—you know, I hadn't even read it. I had to come back to the church and find a copy. So I came down, read it, called her back and told her that wasn't how I saw it. And that it wasn't the kind of thing I'd bring to the council. I just thought you should know."

"Yeah. Well . . . thanks."

But now that I knew: what did I know?

A phone call like that doesn't come out of a vacuum: it really is the tip of an iceberg. People like Mendacia want you to think everyone agrees with them. They may even believe that themselves. But that's never true. Never. It's not unusual to hear council members bring up the same complaint as

The Iceberg

though they're hearing it everywhere, only to find they've all heard it from the same person and no one else.

On the other hand, pastors would like to think that the Mendacias always complain on their own, that one voiced complaint means one existing complaint and no more. That's never true either. Never. (I would say this illusion has a better chance of being true than the other, but then, I'm a pastor.) Mendacia knows and gossips with somebody, many somebodys. There's an iceberg beneath her, ready to rip the hull. A meeting like the one we had only happens because of that iceberg. (Its bulk was revealed by the anger; its limited size by the angry people losing the vote.)

The art of being a pastor involves sensing that iceberg, its size and its location, how to steer around it, how to diminish it, how not to help it grow (while sailing along in the dark).

I had another, stranger, encounter with the iceberg in the same community. This came after a sermon I gave on Memorial Day weekend.

In small Midwestern towns, Memorial Day is a great event. There are ceremonies at all the cemeteries with flags, music, readings, speeches, and rifle salutes. One of the places we served in had an old G.A.R. cemetery on a hill overlooking the valley the town was nestled in: it was quite an experience to march out there with the color guard from the American Legion and the high school band, stand next to the graves of civil war veterans, hear the flags snapping in the wind and look out over the farms and church steeples on the rolling land below. But, good experience or not, if you were a pastor in a small town, you had better show up. All the pastors usually took turns giving a prayer and a blessing.

When I first began serving, you could see Memorial Day as having evolved into a National Day of the Dead. But as the United States became more militarized, especially during the Bush-Cheney years with their "for us or against us" polarization, and the Iraq war went sour, the day became less a day of sorrow and remembrance and more a day of belligerent patriotism.

During that time, if I was giving the sermon the Sunday of that weekend, I would find every serious call of the gospel passage accusing us. I thought the American Christian community had capitulated to earthly power and betrayed itself by the absolute faith it put in military violence.

So I usually tried to raise that still, small voice of peace or at least remind people of the complications of reality. Typically, I would say we tend to remember all the wrong things on Memorial Day and forget how awful wars are, how uncontrollable, how wrong they can go, how soldiers are scarred for the rest of their lives, how leaders and generals always offer the same illusions. I let simple truth be the rebuke.

But they were some of the hardest sermons I wrote, because I felt I had to be so careful, so qualified, if I was going to be understood at all. I had a father who landed at Normandy and a son who served in a Marine Recon Battalion, and I hid behind them shamelessly. I quoted Abraham Lincoln.

People would never say much. If I got comments on those sermons, they tended to be from people who didn't normally say anything, so I tended to value them more. When a man who had his hand blown off in Vietnam told me he appreciated what I said, I didn't care much what anybody else thought.

The encounter I'm thinking about happened in one of the Bush-Cheney years. We had a few visitors Sunday morning, family members in for the weekend, but things went pretty much as usual.

Then, on Wednesday, the local weekly newspaper came out and there was a letter from one of the visitors. He began by praising the Memorial Day ceremony at the cemetery, but the juicy part came next: he was thankful for the ceremony because the church service he had attended the day before was one of the worst imaginable—uninspiring, unpatriotic, virtually a slap in the face to America and its veterans. Or something along those lines.

He didn't exactly name the church or me: but this was a small town even by Minnesota standards, only about five or six hundred people. Everybody knew the family he was visiting and what church they attended. Everybody read the paper, and, if they didn't, someone like Mendacia would show it to them.

Now the strangeness: no one said a word to me. No one. No word, good or bad. The iceberg was completely submerged, brooding on I know not what.

Sunday came. Still the complete silence: it was like a news blackout in a totalitarian country. The event might never have happened.

Wednesday came, with another issue of the paper. Of course, I turned immediately to the Letters to the Editor. And there was a letter from one of our regulars replying to the visitor. After a sharp scolding of this critic from out-of-town (something never to be underestimated in small-town values), he said that, furthermore, I was sometimes the only sensible person he heard talk during any given week.

No one said anything to me about that letter either. Sunday came and went.

The Iceberg

I think it was the next week that I heard the only comment, with one exception, that I was ever to hear about this episode. I was in the library, chatting with the librarian, and, as I got ready to leave, she looked down with a mischievous smile and whispered, "I see your church is getting a lot of free advertising."

I was so tickled that somebody had broken the silence, in a rather neutral manner, that I laughed and lied about how much I enjoyed it. When I left, I realized I didn't know what she thought either.

Here's the exception: a couple of years—yes, years—later, I was in the office on some unremarkable day and one of our splendid volunteers, a smart, commanding woman, a retired nurse and business owner, was using one of the office computers. We chatted often, about all kinds of things, and I must have made some remark that day about the Iraq war.

Without looking away from the computer screen, she said, "If it's any consolation, a lot of people are starting to think you're right."

I was too surprised to say anything. I pondered the phrase "starting to think." She kept working, and we went on to something else. I never really got much more of a glimpse into what people thought.

François Truffaut, the great director, made a wonderful movie called *Day for Night* (*La Nuit Americaine*) about the making of a film. Later in his career, after he had appeared as an actor in Spielberg's *Close Encounters of the Third Kind*, Truffaut said the one thing he hadn't realized when he made his film was that everybody on a film set constantly talks about the director.

When I read that, I thought: if Truffaut hadn't already made some great movies, I'd say he was too stupid to be a film director.

But I would say that about all pastors, without qualification: if you don't know the congregation is going to talk about you constantly, from what you wear to where you shop, you're too stupid to be a pastor. Do something else.

You have to know you are one of the most analyzed elements in congregational life: know it, and then live with it. You won't change it.

The trouble is: it's hard to get an accurate idea of just what exactly anyone is saying. The danger is: knowing that iceberg is there, you can become terrified of it, terrified of its size, terrified of its threat. Some of us fear it more than we should, some of us less.

I think it's one of the things about ministry that most of us are usually wrong about.

Why You Get Phone Calls in the Middle of the Night

Someone's dead.
Someone's dying.
Someone wants to die.
Someone wants you to die.

Passing Through

Both the churches we served the longest were located on the side of U.S. highways. This made them an easy stop for people passing through. Especially when we served our first parish, on the Canadian border, we would get a lot of transients looking for help with food and lodging. It was so isolated up there I'm sure the travellers were desperate sometimes for the mere chance to ask for aid, even directions to a gas station. Also, if you were heading for Canada and looked a little down and out, a little dirtier than a nice Midwesterner should, the Canadian guards would make you prove you weren't completely broke. Someone told me you had to show them at least twenty- five dollars or they'd turn you around and send you back to the States. If you'd already driven all day, you would definitely be looking for help as you came back. There were other churches between ours and the border, but ours was the first on the highway and the parsonage was right next door.

It was late one evening, nearly midnight, and we were locking up and turning out lights, when we had our first encounter with a transient. We heard a knock on the door and, when I opened it, there was a smiling man, about my age, a little stocky, well-dressed. He said, "Sorry to bother you, but—is this the parsonage?"

"Yeah. We're the pastors."

His smile broadened, and he pointed to the church. "I saw the cross there and I knew I could get help somewhere near it. I just crossed the border and I've been driving all day and I can't find any place open around here."

"You won't," I said. "Not this late."

"So I was hoping I could get something to eat." He was a pleasant look- ing guy, he met my gaze, he seemed straightforward. (I'll say immediately: he was. Then I'll add what I learned through the years: the best liars always look that way.)

I said, "Uh—yeah, OK. Come in—we'll see what we've got."

Passing Through

He couldn't have come to a worse place for finding supplies. Our kids always complained that our refrigerator was so empty you might think it had just been delivered. We didn't have that many canned goods on hand either. In our early years, we lived very much hand to mouth.

I think we found a couple of slices of lunch meat, an orange, a scrap or two of something else. My wife was sorting through cans, looking for soup, when our visitor said, "Oh, don't bother with those—you can't tell what they put in them."

He was seated at the kitchen table and, as we brought what we had over, he began peering at each item. His eyebrows went up at the lunch meat. "Not this," he said. "I only eat organic food."

I said: "Oh." But I thought: Man, you knock on a door at midnight in the middle of nowhere and you want to be served an organic meal?

Still, he happily sorted through what we offered and eventually found enough to make a meal of.

He really was a pleasant, engaging person. He told us he was a Roman Catholic and had lived as a brother in a Roman Catholic monastery, though he had left several years ago. He may have been telling the truth. Looking back, however, I have to say that almost all the people that came looking for help told me how much faith they had, how much Jesus meant to them, how important the church was. I should have recorded them for an evangelism training program.

(One woman phoned the church between Sunday services, a woman I'd never met or spoken to, and told me she was moving from South Carolina and was actually *on her way to join our church* when her car broke down—fifty miles away. I think she talked for fifteen minutes about the power of faith before she made her pitch. She wondered if I could wire her a few hundred dollars. When I suggested she look for help a little closer to where she was—instead of asking her if she was out of her mind—she hung up. Never showed up to join the church either.)

But this man was our first wayfaring stranger, arriving early in our service, when we were new, trusting, and idealistic. When he had finished the little we could provide, he thanked us profusely, wished us God's blessing, and went on his way.

It was like getting an easy problem in math for your first day of homework: it makes you think you can do it and that it might even be fun. There was even something extra: I got the story about organic food that I've been telling for thirty years.

The next time I talked to my parents, I told them this story and they made it clear they thought I was crazy for even opening the door, not to mention criminally irresponsible for endangering their grandchildren. (Ten years before this, my father was giving me the same lecture about picking up hitchhikers.) I guess, if I probe my memory, I can't say I even thought about not opening our door or worried much about who would be on the other side. When I did think about it, over the years, I decided opening the door of a parsonage at any time, to whomever might be standing there, should go without saying. I thought that such a minimal response to the unknown was part of who a pastor should be.

I only encountered one person I got a little nervous being around, but that was in the church office and all he cost me was money. I'll discuss him in the next section. But, typically, the people that came to us, while hardly honest, weren't really violent.

Ministerial groups usually have a fund available for transients and for local emergencies. We'd designate the offering from the Thanksgiving service for the fund, but it was never that large; we had to limit what we gave to each request. It was mainly intended for people passing through. There were a couple of local food shelves and, in Minnesota, a lot of assistance was available from the state, if you were a resident. It was the impoverished travellers who knocked at the church doors. We had one checkbook for the fund so that every request went through one person. We'd usually provide a tank of gas and a meal and that was usually what most of our visitors wanted.

We never handed them money; we paid the bill ourselves, and the local restaurants and gas stations would usually be willing to keep a tab for us.

We had a young family stop one evening after they'd been turned back at the border. It was the second time we'd seen them that day. They had stopped earlier to ask if they could use our phone to tell someone in Manitoba they were on the way. They looked pretty spooky. The young man who came to the door was thin and pale. He couldn't meet my eyes. He'd left his car running in our driveway, and I could see at least one other person in the car. I let him use the phone, and they drove off. But they had looked spooky, and the Canadians turned them back. The young man knocked with his wife and child this time, told me what happened and asked if we could find them shelter.

There was a little motel just south of town that didn't do that much business in the winter (once deer season was over). I called them, and the manager said the family could have a room with no charge. He said all the rooms were empty and he was happy to offer help to people that needed it. I gave the family directions and sent them off.

Next morning, I got a call from the motel. The manager said, "Pastor, I know I said I wouldn't charge you, but I have to. They just trashed the place. I'm going to have to replace what they broke. You can come down and look at the damage. I mean—I can't believe you could do that much in one night."

I told him I trusted him, thanked him for the attempt, and said he should send me the bill.

That was an unusual experience. Most people took the little we gave them and went on their way. But the more transients I met, the more it struck me that something had put them on the road, something beyond bad fortune and circumstance, something within that wouldn't let them settle.

One hefty older man walked into my office two days before Christmas. It was snowing outside but, by Minnesota standards, it wasn't that cold. He was very big, towered over me and must have outweighed me by a hundred pounds. He looked even bigger because of all the layers he was wearing and he carried a bulging backpack that he slung to the floor. I wondered why he hadn't left it in his car, so I looked out at the parking lot. I couldn't see a car.

"Did you walk here?"

"I walk everywhere."

"Where'd you come from?"

He told me he'd spent the night in a town about five miles away. I have no idea where he might have started from or if he had any settled residence. For all I could find out, I was looking at all the home he had.

He was a rambling talker, illustrating his tale with cards he would take from his wallet, also bulging, and papers from his backpack. The current section of his journey was taking him from St. Cloud to Fergus Falls, where he said he needed to sign some document related to veterans' benefits.

I said, "And you're walking there." It was a little over a hundred miles.

"Have been. Will be again in a minute or so. Just had a small request."

He wondered if I could let him have the price of a motel room. He told me the town he wanted to get to that night. It was twenty miles north of us.

"Yeah, I can do that. Um—why don't you let me give you a ride there—"

"No, I'll walk."

"It's snowing. Looks like it's coming down harder."

"I walk everywhere."

I called a motel near his destination that I knew had reasonable prices. I asked them if I could make out a check to them for a one-night stay and send it up with a man I was helping. They agreed, which mildly surprised me. I told them he'd be there later in the day.

I made out the check to the motel and told the man it was just for the room so he shouldn't make any phone calls that would be charged.

"Who would I call?"

"Just so you know. Sure I can't give you a ride?"

"Nope."

So I gave him directions and said, "Well, good luck and God bless." We shook hands, he lumbered off into the snow and headed for the highway. I called the motel the next day and they told me everything went well. They thanked me for the business.

His focus on the one thing he wanted wasn't that uncommon, though it was usually about money. There would always be some reason they couldn't take food or a room or even a tank of gas. But if they could just have the money you would have spent on that food, that room, that tank of gas, they'd be fine. In fact, whenever somebody could quickly give me a reason why what I offered wouldn't work, I decided, usually correctly, they would leave me no option but to offer cash, which I wouldn't do. Then they'd walk out without another word.

Another way to sift the wheat from the tares was to offer to contact the sheriff. The sheriff's department is usually aware of all the help that's available in their area and beyond, and it's one of the best places to contact if you really need it. Bringing up the sheriff can clarify how serious the request is.

I got a phone call one morning from a man I eventually figured out was the partner of a woman we'd turned down the day before. (Stories had to be really lame if they couldn't convince gullible people like us.) The man was calling from two towns down the highway, another good test for a phony story. He said he was calling from a motel and needed money to pay his bill and to buy a bus ticket to the Twin Cities. Someone had stolen his car and his wallet had been in the glove compartment.

I said, "Man, why are you calling me? Call the sheriff—they'll get you help. Didn't you report your car was stolen?"

"I can't do that."

(This is where it always got entertaining.) "Why not?"

"Because I know who took it. He's one dangerous dude. Man's a killer."

"OK," I said, "That's an even better reason for me to hang up and for you to call the sheriff. Right now."

"I already told you I can't do that. I guess you just don't understand the code of the street."

It's always fun to hear bad movie dialogue in real life, and I had to swallow my laughter. "You know, I—guess I don't."

"I need that money."

"You need to call the sheriff."

He whined at me a little longer, ridiculing my sheltered existence, but he couldn't find any qualifications in my refusal that he could exploit—something people like my caller are very good at—and he hung up. There's no point in challenging a story like this because all that gets you is more ridiculous conversation: your caller will assume he can satisfy all your objections. Also, he believes he has a chance as long as he keeps you talking; if nothing else, you'll give in to get rid of him.

For the same reason, drifters with flimsy stories will show up or call just before a service is starting. They assume you'll hand them money to get rid of them, since money is quicker than arranging help. I tended to be a little more willing to believe the people who showed up when I wasn't clearly in a time crunch. (But that was before I no longer believed anybody.)

One of the oddest encounters I had was with a family who had a perfectly believable story and who needed very little help. I don't think it could have been more than a full gas tank or some minor engine repair. I can't even remember if we gave them a meal.

All I remember is not being able to make them leave. I can still see this tall, talkative man leaning back against our kitchen sink, his wife standing next to him, and their two children patiently sitting at our table. They were very well-dressed, soft-spoken, apologetic about their need. I remember the man wore a necktie, tidily knotted.

He talked relentlessly: his life, his faith, his views of family, destiny, nature, and civilization. I started timing their presence after they'd been there longer than any transients I'd ever met. They barely deserved to be considered in transit: they were on the verge of being in residence. We were hitting an hour beyond when I checked the clock. I suggested it might be time to arrange for the help he said he needed.

Then he said this: "I'm sorry, but I don't accept charity." (This is the condensed version of a fairly long and extensively illustrated refusal, complete with stern condemnations of those who do accept charity.)

All Hands Stand By to Repel Boarders

I was honestly at a loss for a reply. For a second, I feared I was in something like a *Twilight Zone* episode where someone moves into your house and takes over your life.

I wanted to ask: So what are you doing here? But it struck me that he might need reassurance he wasn't impoverishing us. This was a ridiculous conclusion on my part but, anyway, I said, "Listen: we have a fund set up for this. It's OK. Really. We want to help people if they need a little help on the road."

"I don't take charity. No, sir." He had a southern accent—supposedly the family was on its way to Mississippi—and he spoke emphatically.

We went back and forth like this. I had the weird feeling I had flagged down his car on the highway and was now forcing him to allow me to give him things.

But he had already told me what they needed and I had agreed to give it to them. I just couldn't get him to take it. Finally, I said, "So—what is it you want?"

"Not charity. What you're giving me is not charity: it's going to be a *collaterally secured loan*, which I will give you my solemn promise I will redeem." (I think he added some reflections on the religious concept of redemption.)

I wanted to say: Oh, is *that* all? And then you'll *leave*? What I said, still not getting the point, was: "Oh, you don't have to do that. Like I said: we have a fund for this. We *want* to help people."

"I won't take charity. This will be a collaterally secured loan."

And then I asked the magic question: "OK. I give up. What are you going to offer as collateral?"

"My spare tire and my jack. You keep them, we get home and I send you the money, then you pack them up and send them to me."

(Let's pause to ask: How many pastors, who are not ruthless or insane, are going to take away the spare tire and jack of a family making a transcontinental drive? The answer, known to my visitor as well as to me and to you, is: none.)

And that's all it took. I said I couldn't possibly accept those things when they were making such a long journey. He assured me he was willing to leave them. I assured him he didn't have to.

And so they left, with the same help we had offered them three hours ago, leaving behind the solemn promise to reimburse us. The man made quite a ceremony of copying out our name and address.

I might say: he needed to see himself, and make us see him, as different than someone who came begging. He must have needed to spin out that entire story of his life, since it cost him three hours, too, and he already knew he was getting help. But I think I'd rather put it this way: he needed to feel he was putting something over on us (and here he was more of a common type than he would have believed); he needed to believe he had successfully fooled us, that his story and his cleverness had gotten him something others would have failed to get.

We never saw a penny of his solemnly promised reimbursement. I didn't expect to see it. But he needed to think I did. I started to feel that way about a lot of the people whose stories I listened to: they needed to convince themselves they were fooling me; that was almost more important than anything they got.

The most positive thing I gained from this part of my service was tremendous respect for the social workers who try to dispense help (also from limited resources) to those in need, year after year, who try to make sure their resources go to those who need it most. Anyone who thinks that's easy, or thinks social agencies are too intrusive, should try it.

But what I remember most is what I lost. By the time I retired, if you were a stranger who walked into my office and told me the sun was shining, I'd walk outside and check before I believed you. All the creative stories were wasted on me. You could still get some gas, some food, shelter. I'd even give you a ride to your next stop. But you were wasting your time if you wanted me to believe anything you said.

Mother and Son at Christmas

I WAS AT THE church one Sunday night in December, just before the Sunday School Christmas program. The church was lit up brightly and there was a pretty good crowd. I was in the narthex, happy to be at an event I didn't have a part in, happy we reached this night without the Sunday School teachers strangling each other, when one of the mothers came rushing out of the kitchen, signaling to me.

I walked over and she leaned close to me and whispered, "There's someone on the phone who says he has to talk to a pastor. He says it's an emergency."

I went to the phone. "This is one of the pastors."

It was a deep voice. "Pastor, can I come talk to you? I need to see a Lutheran pastor. It's important."

"Um—sure. Where are you? Can you get to the church?"

"Just down the highway. I can be there in ten minutes."

"I'll meet you at the front door."

Looking back, I should have known something was odd when he asked for a "Lutheran" pastor. If he had the church number, he knew we were Lutheran. It was a subtle way of telling me I was important—unlike, say, a Baptist or a Druid. Subtle, not obvious: he was very good at this.

When he got there, I took him into my office. He was a thick, muscular man, red-faced, with a short beard. He seemed nervous. He asked how confidential our talk could be.

"Completely," I said. "Well—except for two things: if you're on your way to harm somebody or if there's child abuse involved, then there's no deal."

He looked offended. "It's nothing like that." Then he asked if we could lock the door and if he could smoke.

All the drama, I think, fascinated me. I remember being eager to hear what was coming. So I locked the door and he lit a cigarette. I asked him to sit down; he said he'd rather stand. So I sat at my desk while he prowled the office and told me his story.

He needed money. He was on his way to North Dakota, to the farm he had grown up on, to see his mother. She had been quite ill, but it was more than that: she'd been talking about suicide and he was afraid she was serious. He had to get to her. But I shouldn't take his word for it. He handed me a piece of paper with a phone number on it: I should call her.

"No," I said, and this was probably my only intelligent remark of the night, "We'll call the sheriff and they'll get somebody out to her right away."

But no, my visitor said, we couldn't call the sheriff. "That's why I asked you to lock the door. I'm in a little trouble with the law."

This is the point in the story when my older self looks back at my younger self and shakes his head in dismay. If his mother was really *in danger of taking her life*, who would care about his trouble?

As I said, I must have been fascinated by the drama. I would learn, later in the month, I wasn't the only one.

I think I did try to argue a bit, because I remember him backing away a little from the urgency of his claim: he wasn't *sure* she would kill herself, he was only *worried*.

His trouble with the law, on the other hand, was very real. The tires on the car he drove up in were stolen. He blew a tire when he'd started out. He had been frantically worried about his mother and didn't have a spare tire or the money to fix the flat. The big man was almost weeping with frustration, with the bitterness of life. So, as I would phrase it now, he had stolen enough to keep me from calling the sheriff but not enough for me to think it was really all that serious.

Now for the *coup de grace*: he wouldn't have been in the financial mess he was in if his wife hadn't emptied their bank account when she ran off with their pastor. Their Lutheran pastor. He had been sinned against by a member of my tribe.

The only thing I could possibly offer him was money. He would need it for gas and food later. That is, he would need it when he was so far away that I couldn't call the station and expect them to trust me to reimburse them. And he had to be off: it was money or nothing.

Too bad I didn't have much.

I think, too, that even though he had framed his appeal so carefully—mother in peril, prodigal son rushing to the rescue, wounded spouse betrayed by a Lutheran pastor—he must have not quite pushed me over the edge.

So I did what I always did when I was perplexed: I called Ken and asked him what I should do.

I gave him a short version of the man's story. Ken sounded pretty skeptical. He asked me if I believed him.

I sighed. "Oh—"

"Yes and no, huh?"

"Yeah."

But one of the things Ken often said about transients (or anybody that was down and out) was that their being unable to tell you the truth didn't necessarily mean they didn't need help. So he suggested I could give him a little cash—he stressed: a little—and he would reimburse me out of a discretionary fund he had. That way we could help this guy down the road yet limit our damage. Ken said, "If that's not good enough, tell him there's always the sheriff."

I had, unusually, about thirty dollars in my wallet. I took it out and offered it to him. He snatched it quickly, which jarred me a little. Then he stared at it in his hand, eyebrows raised. He waited. I waited.

And then he gave me a disgusted look, stuffed the money in his pocket, wrenched open the door and left without a word.

He had been waiting for me to walk out into the church that was packed with people (as he knew it would be), announce to them that I had a traveller in distress, and take up an emergency collection. When he judged I wasn't going to do that, he left before I had any further thoughts.

How do I know that? I know that because that's what happened in several other churches, not only Lutheran, up and down the Red River Valley that December. I read about it in the Grand Forks paper later in the month. A ministerial group had been bragging among themselves about the help they'd been dispensing during the season—trumpeting their good works in the marketplace, as Jesus might have said—and some one happened to mention the huge collection they'd taken up at church for a troubled man rushing to help his suicidal mother.

Someone else said, "Wait. Not the one whose wife had run off with their pastor—"

A third said, ruefully, "That wouldn't have been the Baptist pastor, would it?"

It was comforting to know my visitor finally met one of the local sheriffs.

I confessed to our own group that I was one of the victims, though I had managed to spare the congregation.

All Hands Stand By to Repel Boarders

Gary, who served the Lutheran church just south of us, asked, "What night was that?"

I told him and he said, "Well, don't feel alone. He'd just come from my office. You know—he was very convincing. I even called that number for his mother. If you can believe this, somebody answered."

"And—"

"She begged me to help her son."

(One of) My Worst Day(s)

When I was on the candidacy committee, one of the seminarians that came through our process was a serious young man who was later called to a church near the one we were serving. This was my third chance to see one of the candidates I'd followed serve as a pastor, and I think Pastor Nathan was the best of the three. I told him once if I'd known how funny he was, I'd have made sure he had an easier time with our committee.

Another young pastor, Pastor Melissa, served in a church between us, and we all covered for each other during vacations or emergencies. It was a good arrangement.

One year, Nathan and his wife were in the process of adopting two children and had to be out of the country for some time. He wasn't aware of any serious needs in his congregation, but we worked out a schedule for us to cover for him week to week.

Everything had been quiet for a few days. Then one morning I got a call from Melissa.

"Is it your turn to cover for Nate?"

"I—think so," I said. "What's up?"

"I just got a call from the hospital. They said they needed somebody to come down for an emergency. I said one of us would."

"What's the emergency?"

"They wouldn't tell me."

I was silent. Melissa said, "Yeah—I know. Um, well, give them a call and good luck." I called the hospital to tell them I was coming and asked what had happened. They wouldn't tell me either.

Pastors get used to walking into rooms or picking up the phone and having a crisis dropped at their feet. But, obviously, you'd rather know what you were heading for. On the drive down, I kept growling to myself about hospitals and privacy. I formulated multiple versions of an ultimatum I would never utter: "Either you tell me what's happened before I walk in that room or I'm going home."

All Hands Stand By to Repel Boarders

It was about a twenty-minute drive. When I got to the nurses' desk, I said I was covering for Pastor Nate and asked what the trouble was. There were several nurses behind the desk. They looked at me blankly, as though we didn't share a language. I think one of them might have told me the room they wanted me to enter. I assumed they were being paralyzed by some guidelines about the order of notification.

I said, "Look. I'd really like to know what's happened before I walk in. C'mon."

One of them finally realized the absurdity of withholding information I would soon have. She took me into an empty room and still had a hard time getting the information out. It struck me then that it wasn't protocol that was silencing them, but sorrow and misery.

A young couple had come in at midnight. The girl was going to give birth. Everything had been on schedule and going well. Sometime during the night, they lost the baby's heartbeat. The child had died in the womb. The couple was alone in the room, the nurses hadn't been able to contact anyone in their families yet, and sometime that morning the girl still had to deliver the baby.

I nodded, thanked the nurse, and walked down the hall.

The room was dark when I opened the door. The boy was sitting on the bed. The girl was propped up, and they were holding hands. I went to a chair on the other side and sat so I could touch them.

They had fallen out of a world of happy expectation, hope, a child's future. They weren't going to get back to it for a long time and, that morning, all we could do was sit there. I could pray, they could tell their story.

We in the church like to talk about the power of presence and the power of words. They seem pretty flimsy when the presence and the words are yours and they're all you've got.

The middle of that day is blurred for me. I went home at some time. Family arrived through the day. The girl delivered the baby. Someone must have asked about baptism; I must have agreed without question. My memory takes me to the evening as we waited for the last of the family to arrive for the ceremony.

The nurses had been doing everything they could for the couple. I think they would have emptied the hospital if they thought it would help. They had brought the baby into the room so the girl could hold it. I was standing just outside the door, talking quietly with someone I didn't know, both of us pretending we were interested in what we were saying. I

(One of) My Worst Day(s)

remember wishing I hadn't quit smoking. I watched older relatives, brothers, sisters, cousins, and friends come down the long hall and shuffle in and out of the room.

At one point, the doctor had to take the baby away for some tests to help them find out what had happened. I was surprised to see it was my own doctor, a woman I'd met my first day in this parish when I sliced my thumb to the bone and had to rush to the emergency room. It was nice, just then, to see someone I knew.

I was with people that night who were being torn in half. They walked into the room, embraced, kissed, looked at the child, cried: all the instinctive gestures of human misery and comfort. Then I watched them exclaim about the child's beauty, wonder who it looked like; they hugged the baby, smiled, cooed, passed the baby to each other with that careful smothering tangle of arms we use because we're terrified of harming a new life. Camera flashes were going off. They were bringing all the welcome and happiness they had been ready to bring, knowing there would be no future to be happy in. Passing by and seeing them, you might not realize the baby was dead.

They weren't acting and they weren't stupid. They were good people who had come to be present, with everything inside them pouring out. I thought I saw more that night of the brave and generous mystery of the human heart than I had ever seen.

We filled the room for the baptism, standing close so we could touch. I led them through the familiar rite. It's a rite of promise, hope, pledges and admonitions but, celebrating it with that stricken family, I saw it was more deeply about communion, love, and belonging.

That's where my memory of that day stops. We've been getting closer and the room beyond is pretty dark. We're nearing the end of the ceremony when we'll run out of scripted words and have to start making up life again. I'm tracing a cross on the forehead of the child, with the father and the mother bent over my hand.

Three of My Failures

First a failure of understanding:

This would have been when I was fairly new, maybe in the first year of service. I was walking to the post office to get the mail one morning, just crossing the railroad tracks. There were never many people around, but that morning a young woman was walking toward me very deliberately. I wondered later if she had been watching for me.

Katie was very pretty, the daughter of a family who farmed just north of town. I think she was either in college or just out of it. She said she wanted to ask me something.

"Do you do elopements? You know, marry people who are eloping?"

It certainly wasn't a question I left the house ready for, so I went a little blank. "Well . . . we usually require several counseling sessions and we really don't want to let those go. Also, there are announcements we have to make in church—we actually have a six-weeks notice requirement. But that's something we can be flexible on. Um—why don't you tell me why you're eloping—"

"Oh, my boyfriend and I just don't want that big wedding circus. We want to do something small and quick."

"Small isn't a problem. I'm not crazy about those circuses myself. We can have a small ceremony, totally private. We'd still want time for those counseling sessions, though. It's good to take some time to talk about being married. It's a big step. Do your parents know you're thinking about this?"

"Oh! Oh, yeah. They're completely for it. We'd just like to do it right away. So—you wouldn't do it right away?"

"Tell you what. You think about it and we can talk again. But we really do require that counseling and it needs a little time. OK?"

Pleasant smile, affirmative nod.

The next thing I heard they had been married by a justice of the peace.

If you guessed that Katie was pregnant and was unwilling or unable to tell me, you understand more than I did that morning. She had probably been putting off approaching me for quite a while, because the baby was born fairly soon.

We did the baptism. I apologized for being dense and assured her we would have done the wedding if we'd known a baby was involved. We would have done the counseling sessions after the wedding, since we also used those sessions as ways to get to know young couples. But I should have understood that I wasn't getting the whole story.

After this, I became a little smarter when people asked me about marriage. The irony is that, had that couple come in for counseling sessions, we would have asked them about pregnancy in our normal set of opening questions. I just wasn't ready for that when I was walking for the mail.

The larger lesson I took from that encounter was never to assume I was getting anything like the whole story, about anything. Even if someone bluntly presents you with a problem, there's often a larger, unmentioned one beneath it that's the real trouble. Finding some way to prolong the conversation and, above all, being silent yourself will often let the truth, or more truth, come out. On the other hand, when someone approaches you in the street, it's probably because they don't want that to happen.

(There's a footnote to this story. About a year later, I was visiting one of our older ladies in the hospital, a pretty shrewd, good-hearted person. She had had some minor surgery and was getting out in a couple days. As our conversation wound down, she said she'd been wanting to ask me something: Was it true I had refused to perform Katie's wedding because I knew she was pregnant? I was aghast that anyone would think this and told her exactly what had happened. She nodded and said it hadn't sounded like something I would do but she wanted to check. Here's another irony: apparently, the person who spread the story meant it as a compliment to me.)

Next, a failure of imagination:

We had just come back, one Sunday, from our second service. It's a time when you're coming down from the intensity of leading worship, greeting people, paying attention to what's going on in the community, and you're looking for silence and for peace. I think I still had my coat on when the phone rang.

It was a woman who wasn't a member of our church but whom I knew from community events. She and two of her friends had gone over to check on another friend named Annie and they had found her dead. Annie had no family in the area and not many connections beyond her group of elderly friends. If she ever went to church, it might have been ours on Christmas Eve or Thanksgiving and, anyway, in that community, our church was where you ended up if you didn't have a church. They had already called the funeral home about the body but they were wondering: would I mind coming over?

This time I had no problem hearing the deeper layer: these nice people had no idea what to do; they felt the dissolving chaos death brings that seems to leave you drifting and directionless; once they called the funeral director, they couldn't leave but they really wanted someone to come and give some shape to the time and space they found themselves in.

"Sure. I'll be right over."

It was a little house, a block away from ours. The woman who had called me answered the door. She led me into the living room and told me Annie was lying in bed. Her two friends were sitting on the couch. They were all wide-eyed, looking at me, and they all looked stunned. I said, "Why don't we say a prayer?" I thought I could feel their relief at being told what to do. So we gathered ourselves into a little circle, let some silence enclose us, and prayed together. Then we talked: first, about what had happened, then about Annie herself, how they knew her, what they knew of her life. The funeral director, whom I knew well, came: a kind, quiet man, he brought a gentle presence to that hard, grim fact of taking away a body that simply can't be left to decay where it is. Then we dispersed.

After the funeral, a couple of days later, the woman who had called on Sunday took my arm, thanked me, and said she'd always remember me coming over to be with them.

I remember, too. It's a memory I cringe at because I failed to do the most important thing: I failed to take them into the bedroom to gather around Annie and say our last prayer around her, with her. At the moment I walked in the door, I didn't have the imagination to see that death had repelled them. They weren't simply sitting in a different room: they were frozen there. I let their immobility stop me. More importantly, I didn't have the imagination to see that life was still hovering around Annie's body and that it needed to be honored, not ignored.

I should have gone straight to the body, acknowledging that life. I should have taken everyone with me and said our prayers there. It still bothers me that I failed to do that, but I never made the same mistake again.

Finally, a failure of attention and will:

We woke one day to wailing sirens, heading south of town. A little later in the morning, we heard there'd been a terrible accident involving

Three of My Failures

a young man from our congregation, from a family we knew pretty well. Someone had been killed and he had been thrown from his car. He was hurt so badly they were rushing him to the hospital in St. Cloud.

So I got my prayer book and my coffee thermos, and I started off down the highway. This was near the end of my service. By now, cell phones—those blessings to all of us who traveled the lonely country roads—-were in common use. Oddly enough, if I hadn't had mine with me, or if I hadn't had it on, I might not have failed the way I did.

I was some way down the road when I got a call from the hospital chaplain. He had called the church and got my number from the office: he asked if I was on my way down.

When I said I was, he said: "You might want to rethink that. They're going to fly him to Minneapolis, and the family's getting ready to take off. There's no telling how things are going to go and—maybe you want to wait for things to be a little more settled before you make that trip."

The young man's parents were with the chaplain, and he handed the phone to them. We talked a little, but they were on the way out, and the father said something like, "So you're probably not coming down right now."

I said something like, "I guess not."

I should have kept going. Period. I should have simply assumed I would catch up with them somehow. I let what the chaplain said stop me. But it was my decision, my failure: I should have kept going.

What has bothered me most about this is that I usually made myself make the trip, make the visit, make the call. I hated putting things off. If you had asked me the night before what I would do in a situation like that, I would have said: I would keep going. If you asked me today what I would typically do in a situation like that, I would say: I would keep going.

But I didn't.

As I've thought about this, I've wondered if it was a question of fatigue, of feeling overwhelmed, if I was too tired to brush aside the chaplain's word of caution. There are times when problems or tasks you deal with routinely seem almost impossible. You're simply exhausted, overloaded. The slightest obstacle stops you in your tracks.

I don't know if that was my problem that morning. Anyway, those are realities, not excuses. The important point, I think, is that, in a case like this, you can't allow the fatigue to make the decision for you. You have to push through it. Realize you're tired, make a commitment to take time off, take that time, but on that morning: keep going.

It doesn't matter how effective you are when you get there. Unless you can work miracles, you'll never be effective enough anyway. Being there is the important thing.

Now here's the worst part: when I finally got down to the hospital, most of the family were gone; when I tried to find them in town, they'd be on the road; when I'd make the hospital trip again, they would be somewhere else. Messages were left, missed. It seemed like forever before I could talk to them face to face. It became one of those situations where you can never seem to do the right thing, be in the right place, find the right word: you're always stumbling. You always seem to be coming in too late and out of step, but the real problem is you should have been there at the beginning, and you weren't. If you had been there at the beginning, later lapses wouldn't matter.

The young man did live and come home. The last time I saw him, he was still using a cane. But I never saw that family again without accusing myself of letting them down.

If there's one moment of my service I'd like to have the chance to live again, it's the moment I stopped my car that morning and turned back.

Trying to Go On

We were doing a wedding on a terribly hot summer day. In those days, no one in northern Minnesota thought of air-conditioning a church as anything but a grotesque luxury, suitable only for Episcopalians. We had set up some fans for the wedding party, but the church was full, the humidity was high, and it was getting pretty uncomfortable. During one of the musical numbers, I heard a rustle and a thud to my left. One of the groomsmen had fainted. He cracked a tooth on our wooden communion rail as he fell, leaving a chisel-shaped dent in it.

(There are wrenching continuities and contrasts in parish life: we did this boy's funeral not that long a time later, after he was killed in a car wreck, and I pointed out the dent during the sermon. Some of the family had already gathered around it, before the service, reminiscing, touching part of his life.)

I looked over that afternoon and saw him on the floor, a groomsman on either side of him, looking down. Before I could wonder what to do, they smiled at each other, picked him up, carried him to an empty pew, and returned to their places, closing the gap between them. I doubt if people in the back of the church even knew anything had happened.

That was an easy one, but it illustrates almost all the essential things that have to happen when there's some sort of emergency or when, for whatever reason, that wonderful order of the ritual starts to unravel around you: don't even try to pretend nothing's happened; make sure the problem is being addressed by someone; get back to what you were doing.

I have two examples of trying to pretend nothing's happened that I was involved in before I was ordained.

Before we went to seminary, I was on the music and worship committee of the little church we were part of. It was a university town so, when school was in session, there was a lot of musical talent around. We often had student organists who, reasonably enough, wanted to go home for the holidays. This left us looking for substitute organists when there were few to be found.

One year, the only person I could find was a grad student in chemistry who was a pretty good amateur keyboard player but who had never played for a church service. At that time, the LCA used a service book with two very traditional services: one with texts set to repeating tones which shift according to breaks in the lines and syllables; the other based on a Swedish mass setting built on Gregorian chant. The second would be easy to play for anyone who read music. The first, however, while looking like music, with whole notes, half notes, quarter notes, is not timed to beats but to the words themselves. This sounds harder than it is until you've heard it: then you see its simplicity. But if you've never heard it or seen the notation, it's difficult to get the sense of how it goes.

We had been using the Swedish mass setting, so I went through it with my substitute the week before she was going to play: the setting, as well as the hymns, were well within her ability.

Sunday morning came, she was there on time, we went through the service together again, she began the prelude, I went to sit with my family.

That was my first mistake. The organ was in the choir loft at the back of the church, and I should have stayed there, in case there was a problem, a question. But that wasn't my biggest mistake. That came next.

The pastor walked out to greet everyone and, as we were about to start, he said, "Oh, let's shake things up—let's use the first setting today."

Horrified at the wreck of all my preparation, I looked at my wife, rolled my eyes and headed for the organ loft. When I got up the steps, the organist was dutifully turning pages to find the first setting. She reached it just as I came up behind her. She stared for a second at the music, then looked up at me and said, "I have no idea how to play this."

Here's what I did, and I thought I was rising wonderfully to the challenge: I whispered a quick description of how the music was intended to go, chanted a little of it in her ear, while everyone wondered what was happening in the organ loft, then told her I would sing along next to her. Thus, we limped through the service.

I was being an idiot. Here's what I should have done: as soon as the pastor announced the change of setting, I should have headed for the altar, not the organ, and told the pastor that, since we had a substitute (which he was well aware of), he simply couldn't change musical settings. Period. Instead, I tried to make it seem as though nothing had happened.

My second example is more serious but it too involves a kind of imprisonment by formality.

Trying to Go On

This was during my internship year. Again, it was a church where the organ was in the choir loft, making communication difficult. The regular organist was excellent, but the church had several organists and one of the regular substitutes was playing that day. We had sung the first hymn. I was chanting the assisting minister's part, so I was at the altar, waiting for the organist to give me the first note of the *Kyrie*. I could see her poised at the keyboard, looking at the music. I waited. No note.

I looked at the pastor and he signaled me to begin without it. So I picked a note, sang my line, and waited for the organist to lead the congregation in. I had my eyes on her: she still sat as though frozen. So the pastor led the singing unaccompanied.

Then I saw the organist slide off her bench and disappear under the organ. She was up again before I could wonder how I ought to react to that, and she began paging through her music. I was getting more and more rattled. Just as I was thinking we would probably do the service without music, the organist began to play. But she had lost all sense of where we were in the service and was simply flipping pages, playing whatever piece of the liturgy she landed on.

Here's what I mean by being prisoners of formality: nobody did anything, nobody said anything; nobody made that miserably short trip to the choir loft to see if maybe they could help out. We all pretended we were doing a normal service.

As the congregation was leaving, someone whispered to me, "Well, you got your initiation with Sadie." I thought: this happens a lot? When all had left, the pastor told me a little about her: that she was troubled, going through a divorce, taking medication that she would sometimes omit, sending herself out of control. Even apart from that, she could be a difficult person.

But why did that mean we ignored what was happening? I can't exempt myself from the general failure. It never occurred to me or, apparently, anybody else, that we might have done more than let the organist flounder alone for an hour. We were so imprisoned by our formality that we couldn't even think our way out of it.

Looking back on that day, after my own time of service, I am aghast that no one did anything. I think it was a combination of an extremely formal community, a person with a known history of problems, the fact that it was the organist in that distant perch, and that the disturbance was not a person collapsing but the organ playing with no connection to anything that brought about an initial paralysis. It wasn't like someone fainting in the pew in front of you. There was, immediately, no instinctive impulse to follow. There seemed to be, immediately, no reason to act. But when no one acted immediately, it became harder to act at every second, and we played out this grotesque charade.

But, explain it as we might, we were wrong to pretend nothing was happening. When it was clear the problem was serious and wasn't going to solve itself, someone should have broken ranks and done something. If you're leading worship, the someone of last resort is you.

In my own service, there are two incidents of sudden illness that I recall, one fairly mild, the other fairly frightening.

The first happened in the first parish we served. The church was in a town near a state park and, during the summer, we had several regular visitors who would worship with us during their vacations.

One summer, a very pleasant elderly couple had been coming for a few weeks. They would sit close to the front, near the lectern. I think I had just asked the congregation to rise for the reading of the gospel: they stood, the man coughed and reached for his throat, then began to fall.

There's an outcry you hear when a crowd is shocked and concerned, a collective "oh!" as its first response. But the man didn't fall far. He was sitting right in front of the Fire Department Chief, who caught him and eased him down. An EMT who served as the town's first responder was sitting two rows back. She had all her equipment in her car, and she was on her way to get it as the chief was loosening the man's tie. So there was no problem in getting immediate attention. (And, as it turned out, there was nothing serious wrong.)

The problem was occupying everyone else. If you have a good view of a crowd when something like this happens, you can see them leaning in, drawing close, as though the distressed person is physically pulling them. But the last thing that person needs is to be smothered by people who may want to help, or think they should help, but really have no help to give. You have to guide their attention elsewhere.

I think you can say about a case like this what is always said about justice: it not only needs to be done; it needs to be *seen* to be done. The person must be helped; then everybody else has to know help is being given.

We let people know the EMT was working, then we used that powerful church call to order: "Now let us pray . . . " We said a prayer together, announced the EMT and the Fire Chief would handle things from there, and went on with the service.

It was another time I was lucky in the people who were on the scene.

In the last incident I'll discuss, I wasn't so lucky and the collapse wasn't so mild.

While we were serving our last parish, we were also doing a long part-time interim at another parish that was in the process of calling a pastor. We had been doing this for a few months, so we were getting to know the congregation, but it was still a little like being a regular substitute. You weren't that familiar with the community, your position among them wasn't that solid, you felt a little more on your own.

One Sunday, I was in the middle of my sermon, and I thought it was going fairly well. The church was built as a kind of amphitheatre, the pews flaring up and out from the chancel area, and it was reasonably full. Then a big man sitting in the very front of the congregation stood up. Russ was one of our regulars, well known, well liked.

I kept going but, in an arena like that, any sudden, out of place movement will draw every eye in the room. Russ moved along his pew, heading for the aisle, while I talked on and watched everyone else watch him. He headed up the aisle, heads turning with him. He had one hand pressed to the side of his head.

He had just reached the very last row of pews, and I was hoping everyone's attention would drift back to me, when he stopped, swayed, and fell straight down with no attempt to break his fall. The congregation cried out as he hit the floor. He didn't move.

My memory of that moment is of a kind of frozen tableau: every person in the room is turned toward the body on the floor; he fell so fast, so suddenly, he's lying so motionless that no one moves, they're stunned; I see all this from my privileged view in the pulpit; I'm the only one standing up, but all I'm aware of is the scene; I'm not even aware that I've stopped talking. I do remember that my first thought was: "NOW what?"

I saw one of the ushers moving toward the fallen man, so I said something like, "OK, we're going to let the ushers see what's happening and the rest of us are going to pray right now." I went into one of those impromptu psalm-like prayers where you state obvious truths: we don't know what's going on, we don't know what to do, we're looking for light, help, and rescue. While I spoke, I saw the usher leave and then return, signaling me.

I wrapped up the prayer and nodded to him. He said Russ was coming to, but they were going to keep him lying down. The paramedics were on the way.

Since this wasn't my home community, I had no idea where they were coming from. I thought singing a few hymns would give us a flexible strategy, so I asked the organist if she could play some while we waited. As she walked to the organ, I led another prayer, and then we sang hymns: all the brave shouts of faith in times of woe—Amazing Grace, Abide with Me, Children of the Heavenly Father, I Know That My Redeemer Lives. After a lifetime of funeral planning, all the old ones presented themselves to me one by one, and we sang until the paramedics came, worked on Russ, and began to take him out. I cut off the hymn, we had another prayer, and we ended with the Lord's Prayer.

And then we went back to what we were doing. I did a quick improvised ending of my sermon, in light of what we'd just been through and the uncertainty of what would happen to Russ. And then we entered what seemed to me at the time the most powerful and redemptive path we could take: the ancient words and actions of the communion service, that ritual drama that sums up the Christian's journey.

I saw Russ in the hospital shortly after the service, and then out and about the next week, grumbling because he wasn't supposed to drive. The last I heard, he was still in that frustrating medical drama of tests and inconclusive results which now is part of the earthly journey for so many of us.

Before I went to the hospital, though, I stood at the back of the church as I usually did, shaking hands with the congregation, doing the pastor's survey of the state of the community. I got lots of squeezed hands, hugs, whispered thanks.

But all I really did was hang on and find a way to keep doing what we had come there to do: worship and pray as a Christian community. Everyone was more than ready to follow me. Walking in that morning, we already had the most powerful way of getting us through what would happen: all the meditation on the perils and losses of life compressed in Christian hymnody, prayer, liturgy. We just had to remember that and find our way back to it.

Raging at the Dead

We were doing the funeral of a young man who died much too early in life. I heard he had lived recklessly, but I didn't know him, and people are always looking for reasons to distance misfortunes they don't want to think about. He came from a small family, his parents were gone, and his closest relative was his sister, who had to fly in from California.

In our tradition, family members, as the chief mourners, process into the church at the beginning of the service. We were lined up to begin, the funeral director and his assistant were ready with the casket, the organist was finishing the prelude, and the sister was gone. We looked outside, we looked in the kitchen, someone checked the restroom. Then I heard a voice coming from my office, sharp, angry, barely controlled, getting louder. I walked in. She had her back to the door and was starting to scream into the phone. She had called the florist's shop and was raging at them about the shabby flowers they had provided for her brother's funeral.

There was nothing wrong with the flowers.

She had battled about everything when we were planning the service. The funeral director told me he had the same experience with her: nothing pleased her, she claimed he always misunderstood what she selected, his prices were ridiculous.

She raged at everything around her because the only person she wanted to scream at couldn't hear her anymore, the brother who had left her alone. She wanted to rage at death, for being a reality; at life, for being short; at herself, for being wounded, powerless, alone. But there is nothing more silent than the simple nature of things, nothing more crushing.

Another time, we were doing a funeral that should have been one of those peaceful ceremonies at the end of a long life, the laying to rest of a matriarch, blessed with many good years, children, grandchildren, someone beloved by the community.

We went to her home to plan the service with her four children. Usually, this took an hour or so, and this was a busy time for us, so we had already scheduled another meeting for later in the day.

We ended up leaving them, over two hours later, with very little planned, a promise from them to settle things, and another appointment the next day. They argued about readings, about hymns, about who had the right to choose what. They told elaborate stories to show that someone's choice would be an insult to someone else. They agreed more on what could not be in the service than on what could. There were tears, fists striking the table, people storming from the room, doors slamming.

It was one of the longest funerals we ever did. There were more congregational hymns and more vocal solos than we usually had, but that wasn't the reason for the length. One of the siblings had lost most of the battles about the music, but they agreed he could speak on behalf of the family.

Once he got warmed up, I'm sure the rest of them wished they had given him anything else. I usually advised people to write out their remarks and to keep them short. But he spoke without notes, and after twenty minutes I stood up and walked to the lectern. I put my hand on his arm and whispered, "You should probably wrap it up."

To that point, his speech hadn't been that bad. He nodded to me and said, "Sure, sure."

So I sat down again. I suppose he thought it was now or never, and he began to settle the scores of a lifetime, unveiling every slight, every hurt, handing out blame to his sisters like the recording angel run amuck. I wonder now if they were impressed by how much he remembered. It was an eerie tirade because he never raised his voice. He looked calm, peaceful. If you couldn't hear what he was saying, you would marvel at his composure. Then he began accusing his sisters of failing to care for their mother, virtually blaming her death on them. I stood up again. On my way across the chancel, I saw one of the sisters curl up in the pew and begin sobbing.

This time I gripped his arm and said, "That's it. You have to stop. Right now." I took a step back, but if he didn't stop, I thought I'd pull him away from the microphone and lead him back to his pew. I wondered how that would go.

He finished quickly, smiled, nodded to me, and walked back to sit with his family. They had spent days, and would probably spend more days, arguing about and raging at everything but the great thing: death had come among them and their mother was gone.

The shadow of death falls over people differently, unpredictably. It really is like feeling a blow in the darkness and trying to find some way to strike back.

Raging at the Dead

Often enough, it's the pastor who becomes the target of those raging emotions. I weighed every word when I wrote funeral sermons. I would spend hours phrasing them and be dripping with sweat when I finished. You want to speak the truth about the life ended; you want to do it with love; you want to do it without provoking more grief, anger, misery. With certain lives, certain families, things done and especially things left undone, that will be a thankless, and sometimes hopeless, task.

I would look up at the Samuel Beckett quote on the shelf over my desk: "Try again. Fail again. Fail better."

Death will always shake people up in ways beyond imagining. You simply have to know that and live with that.

Once the rage flared up inside me.

It was the dying and the funeral of another young man, but one I knew very well. He was in my daughter's high school class and was one of the most talented actors and singers the school had ever seen. He went away to college, then moved to New York with high hopes for a career in the arts. He'd come home often and one year we acted together in community theatre. He played Captain von Trapp and I played Max in *The Sound of Music*.

Then one Sunday he showed up in church, home for a visit, and I barely recognized him. He was shockingly thin, with sunken cheeks, and I thought he looked feverish. I think I blurted out something like, "What's wrong? Have you been ill?"

He laughed dismissively and said he liked to stay thin because it was easier to put on weight for a part than to take it off.

I didn't believe it. As we shook hands, I caught a slight smell from him that seemed strange, troubling, a smell from hospital rooms of the seriously ill. A few months later, he came home to die and never made it. He collapsed at the airport and was taken straight to a hospital.

No one ever said the word "AIDS" out loud. But when people did speak or inquire about him, you could tell they thought it. I didn't see much point in asking.

When I visited him in the hospital, I had to wear protective clothing, including a mask, to protect him from infection. One of the things I remember most is how inexpressive I felt.

He was on life support, but there was no kidding anybody about his condition. He had too many things wrong with him beyond the reach of treatment: infections spreading, organs failing, tissue decaying. There was a kind of gentle movement within the family to a point where they could let him go.

All Hands Stand By to Repel Boarders

Sometimes, when you visit, those who have been keeping vigil can use your presence to take a break: get lunch, run an errand, just leave the room for a time. So I was sitting alone with him one day, talking about all kinds of things in a rambling way. He was pretty weak, we drifted into silence.

I was sitting there looking at the wreck of this beautiful person. I can't remember now what I was thinking, what moved within me. But, being alone with him, I was suddenly filled with fury, and I got an overwhelming urge to grab him and shake him, pound him against his pillow, and scream, "How dare you cause all this grief! How dare you bring all this misery on your mother! How dare you!"

How dare you leave us, the people who love you, who watched you grow, sent you off with hope. How dare you let death take you away.

The rage passed. I knew enough by then to know what it was about: nothing but loss and being powerless.

I've choked up at a lot of funerals, but his is the only one I completely broke down at. It was a big funeral: we had asked to use a larger church in town to accommodate the crowd, and it was packed. You're choking on the grief before you start.

We always read a brief obituary before the lessons. I began it but only got as far as the year he was born, 1968, the same year my daughter was born. My voice broke, I tried to go on, but couldn't get another word out. I looked up at the congregation, many of whom had been sobbing from the moment they walked in. I held my hands out, pleading for I know not what, then stood there and helplessly cried.

When I could stop, I went on. The service went on. Life went on. No matter what you say, do, or feel, the boy is still dead and death is still waiting for the rest of us.

The Emptiest Word in the English Language

Forever. As in: live forever; love forever; live forever in memory; love you forever.

Hebrew is more honest: all you can say is "for a long time." But that helps you hear how silly it sounds, doesn't it?

PART FIVE

Flesh

In the last year I served, a young woman I'd known since she was in high school told me she needed to talk to me. Ellie had been going through bad times, in work, in life, finding herself too close to the wrong person in the wrong relationship, problems not of her making. She thought her life was on the mend, and she wanted to ask me about a decision she had to make. I don't think she wanted my advice, only a friendly ear. I also don't think I could have talked here out of her decision; but she'd be happy if I thought it was a good one.

She wanted to show me her life and have me see the same person I saw ten years ago, before things went so bad.

Ellie was a bright, talented, responsible person. She had spotless skin, that pale Nordic beauty that looks smooth and polished, unreal. But the healthy flesh held a troubled spirit.

We talked for an hour or so. She seemed good to me. I thought she could see hope in her life. But it's easy to be wrong about people, especially about the people you like.

I thought we'd end our talk with a prayer, so I reached across the table and took her hand. She still had that smooth, pale, unwrinkled skin. Her fingers were a little short, a little pudgy. My hand was dark, thin, marked up, a little crooked from getting twisted in a drill and broken years ago.

And, as I took her hand, seeing the different years of our human journey pictured so graphically, I suddenly had an unnerving series of images flooding out of my memory, all the hands I'd held in the prayers of thirty years. The vision came so suddenly and was such a surprise I think I might have gasped out loud.

I was probably feeling my age that morning. I was probably feeling upset by some of the things Ellie had told me, sorry for her pain, hoping for better. Maybe I was a little vulnerable to something like this. But that moment is burned into my memory: I see Ellie sitting before me, I see our hands, I've finally collected myself enough to begin praying, and right between us there is hovering another pair of hands, from one of the first hospital visits I made to someone slipping toward death. Another woman, but at the other end of life.

Some spark ignited by the flesh had carried me back to the beginning of all this.

It was when I was on internship. I had made hospital visits before, but I had never been so physically close to someone so emaciated, burned up from within by whatever was killing her.

There was so little left inside her I could see her veins and her bones, the flesh withering around them. They looked like you could pluck them out of her with one finger. I thought of the pictures I'd seen of prisoners from the camps of the Second World War: people whose muscles were so far gone they couldn't raise themselves.

I took her hand to pray. Mine was the young flesh, bright and full. But she gripped me as though her life could be saved by hanging on. It was probably a spasm of pain. It was certainly a demonstration that I could never give what the desperate wanted.

That memory will never leave me either. I remember some of the thoughts I had in its wake working their way into my sermons: the claim the flesh of others makes on us; our flight from our kinship with the diseased; the mirror offered to us by suffering flesh, the mirror of our future, our nature, our fate.

Those thoughts would always rise up when I'd have to preach on Jesus curing the lepers, Jesus raising Lazarus. So much of his power and his message is carried by his physical presence, his physical touch. He's comfortable in the twilight where boundaries dissolve, where the illusions of the fortunate disappear. The touch of Jesus, given to all, shows his fearlessness, his transgressive availability, his threat. (He doesn't even respect graves. He opens them.) He touches the diseased. He touches the dead.

He made that fearless facing of human decay and fleshly distortion part of the path Christians are called to follow.

Because of where I served, I spent a lot of my days in hospitals and nursing homes, among the sick, the marred, the aged, the dying. There were times I would find myself thinking I was years older than I really was. Very little in my own real aging has surprised me. Also, I saw enough horrors to make me thankful every day I can stand up.

There's one more touch of flesh I won't ever forget.

One of the families we knew pretty well carried an unfortunate heritage of multiple sclerosis. My visiting rounds took me often to the mother who was still able to live at home, though not for long, and a daughter who lived in a nursing home. Then another daughter, Cindy, who had moved away, was stricken and came back to the area, moving to the home her sister was in. I got to know her just a bit before she moved on again, to a nursing home that was nearer her children. She was, at the time, understandably depressed, bitter, a little touchy. Especially at first, I had to choose my words with care.

Then, a few years later, I got a call from Margie, the social worker at one of our other nursing homes. Cindy was back again, having had a terrible time and very poor care in the home she had gone to. The social worker asked if I would drop in on her soon. I said I would.

Then she said, "But come see me before you do. Don't go to her room without talking to me first."

Well ... OK.

The day I went, I found Margie in her office and asked her what was up. She told me Cindy had contracted a painful, raging skin virus that needed constant care. The sores covered her entire body, from her head to her feet. Margie had wanted to prepare me for what she would look like and also to assure me there was no danger of contagion. I wouldn't need any more protection than I would normally use in a hospital. I could take her hand to greet her or to pray, if I wanted.

I confess as I walked down the hall to Cindy's room my heart was beating a little faster and I found I was taking some deep breaths. I could see her door was open as I turned into her hall. Cindy was looking up at the ceiling, unaware of my approach, so I stopped short of the door to get myself settled.

It's one thing for somebody to tell you how bad a shape someone is in. It's quite another to see that person in the flesh, flesh you would pray would never be yours or anyone's you loved, flesh you were approaching and could not turn from without betraying what you said you believed in. It's one thing to be told there's no danger of contagion.

I stood there, hesitant, and the image of Jesus, the man who cured the lepers, rose up and rebuked my lack of faith.

So I walked into the room. Cindy turned. My heart was in my throat. "Hey, Cindy," I said, "Remember me?" I smiled and put out my hand to shake hers.

Breath

I was out visiting one day at the farm of a man who was dying about ten feet from where he'd been born almost a century before. I said, at his funeral, that if someone had tied a long enough rope around his ankle the day he was born, he might never have noticed it was there. I was sitting with his wife and a young woman from the neighboring farm. The man was leaving the earth in his own measured way, so we were in the time of keeping vigil, the expanded moment of waiting for the end, still a few days distant.

I can't remember what provoked the remark, but we must have been speaking of last moments when the young woman said, "Oh, but—you must have been with people when they died."

Her eyes were bright, inquisitive. Her remark—with the implied question: "So what's it like?"—surprised me a little. For one thing, I often forgot how familiar I was with things other people never saw. But it was the kind of thing I got most often from confirmation students, who would ask bluntly what it was like. It's tempting to scorn questions like this, and I know many do, as though they show a kind of morally impure curiosity. This strikes me as a way, perhaps understandable itself, of feeling superior from the simple fact of having experienced something miserable. But I think it's as natural to be curious about life's end as about life's beginning. So I always told them what little I knew.

All the deaths I watched over were peaceful, known to be approaching, often prayed for as the clear time to die had come. So my experience of death has its own bias. They were departures, not battles to remain. Still, the body yields slowly and it's the breathing I remember, listening to the breaths, the gasps, hearing the rhythm jerk, pause, rush, stop, begin again. Then it stops and, always, for a second or two, I waited for the next one, until I realized it wouldn't come. Breathing, then not: it's at once the simplest thing and the strangest thing. I often thought of a remark by Randall Jarrell: you felt, looking at the dead, the way people felt on first reading Wordsworth's poetry: it was so simple you couldn't understand it.

Breath

In the hospital once, I was sitting with a man's large family in his room. The staff didn't think he'd last the day. He was lying peacefully while we talked around him, over him. They were a large family that enjoyed each other. It was a happy sound and I thought it wasn't a bad way to end life.

All of a sudden, the girl sitting on her father's right said: "I think he's gone!" And he was, so quietly no one heard.

But sometimes the last breaths seem to be dragged from the air with all the effort the weak body can make, wheezing like a laboring pump, the body tensing with each breath, then sagging. It seemed less a struggle made than a torture inflicted. It's not the easiest thing to listen to.

Then it stops. Sometimes there's a cough, a gasp, a sigh, a moan; sometimes not. Breathing, then not. I thought I could feel the life dropping away: not down, or up, but somehow back into some other dimension, away from the rest of us. Once, I had such a strong sense of this I thought I could reach out and put my hand right through the body and grab the departing life and pull it back. I had probably been sitting there too long.

Simple and strange: all at once, something right in front of you has stopped, someone is still. An absence has appeared before you, a body suddenly still, motionless. It's as simple and as strange as that.

I remember one death more vividly than the others. It was late at night, in a dark, quiet care center, and I was the only other person in the room.

The woman I was sitting with, Grace, was over a hundred years old. She was already a resident in the care center when I met her, years before that night, already older than anyone else I knew. She was a bright, great-hearted, unfailingly pleasant person, a lifelong nurse and caregiver. With a few more people like Grace, the world would have a lot less to worry about.

She was from a large family, and I knew two of her sisters. They were widows who lived together after their husbands, two brothers, died. They were elegant ladies whom I first noticed because they sat on the pulpit side at church, just about in the center of my view, and they were always dressed glamorously. But they really stood out for me because of one of those mental errors you never forget. I asked someone what their names were: the person I asked mumbled something like "Oh, those are the Twisted Sisters" and hurried away, leaving me to think of them, helplessly, as The Twisted Sisters from that moment on.

(They were lovely people as well. When the eldest was dying a few years after Grace, I remember looking out her living room window with her, watching a couple of squirrels chase each other in the yard. She sighed and smiled at me and said, "This is such a beautiful, fascinating world." I agreed but, while she was thinking of the squirrels, I was thinking of her.)

Grace was getting close to the end so the sisters asked us, one day at church, if one of us could be there when it came. They were quite frail themselves and no longer drove at night, but they hated to think of Grace dying alone. We said we certainly could and they left word at the care center to call us.

I think it was going on eleven o'clock one night when I took the call. Nurses will react at different speeds to different degrees of urgency but, after some gentle probing, I thought it was time to be there. I got my Occasional Services book and left.

It was strange to pull into the parking lot, always so full when I visited, and be able to park near the entrance. It was strange to enter the darkened hallway without trading wisecracks with the office staff or greeting the residents who haunted the entryway. I walked to the main nurses' station and said I was there to be with Grace.

She was still fairly lively, at least conversationally, when I first knew her. She would light up when you walked in the door, then, as she tired, she would take your hand and tell you it was so nice of you to come. Over the years, the moments between grew shorter until all that was left was the spark of greeting and the gracious dismissal.

I could hear her gasping as I reached her door. She was propped up a little in her bed, lying fairly still, not really conscious of my entrance, face turned upward, mouth slightly open, and breathing in labored, drawn out, whistling breaths, like a child choking to death, yet not thrashing about, nearly motionless, nearly gone. I sat on her right, close enough to take her hand.

For these moments, I had some prayers and psalms I would go through, with others or not, aloud or not, to mark the time. Grace hadn't stirred at my touch: her life had come down to the struggle for breath. I spoke my service quietly and settled to wait. I listened to her breathe, second by second, minute by minute.

The room had only a weak, indirect light above the bed. The corridor was empty and it was a long way to the nurses' station. Grace and I sat there together in the dark. I stared at the second hand on the clock across the room and listened to her struggling for air.

It's a powerless feeling. You want to ease the breathing somehow. You want, I suppose, to see her smile again, you want her life not to be ending.

Breath

You might as well go all the way back and wish none of us had ever been born.

And then it came to me: I could end this. She was going to die before dawn and I could spare her all those struggling hours. The pillows were large and thick. Her weak body couldn't fight me off. I could pray over her, bless her, cover her face with the soft pillow, and give her peace. It would be over in a moment, in the twinkling of an eye.

I'll probably never forget that thought entering my mind, how much sense it seemed to make in the quiet dark.

I didn't even have to assure myself no one would know. I knew no one would know. By that time in my life and service, I thought that ending suffering, for once, rather than watching more of it, wouldn't bother me much, though I might have been wrong about that.

I can't even say I was struggling with the thought. It was just sitting inside me while I sat next to Grace. It was there as one thing I could do in the next minute or so, along with getting some water or saying more prayers or continuing to sit there doing nothing. I suppose it was moral inertia, something I by no means scorn, that made me continue to sit and do nothing.

But, looking back, I think if I had done it, I would simply have risen and done it, with no struggle at all. If the night, my vigil, listening to the pained breathing, had been long, it's possible I would have.

But, soon, the next breath did not come. I put my hand on Grace's head, said a farewell prayer, recited the Nunc Dimittis and blessed her, tracing a cross on her forehead.

I checked the time and walked down the corridor to tell the nurse.

Sorrow

Every once a while, there would be a cluster of deaths and the church would be doing funeral after funeral. In the second parish we served, we did over twenty funerals in our first year. One gruesome January, when we were temporarily serving two different churches sixty miles apart, we would be doing one funeral in the morning on Monday and meeting with another family in the afternoon to plan the service for Thursday. Thursday afternoon we would meet with another family to plan the next.

You get trapped within the grief. Whenever it comes, however it comes, Death calls us out of the ordinary into its own world, and sometimes that's a gift, a great gift: we leave the trivial and come to the essential. We sit in silence in the room of the dying and we are simply there, together, within the bond of love, without distraction.

But if you're there too long, too often, you die to everything else. You lose interest in everything else. You live in the night vigils, the old memories, the wordless touches, the gathering of family and friends, the whispers of the hopeless verdicts, the search for words to speak.

I remember, during one of these periods, paging through album after album of photographs, then realizing, weeks later, that every time I saw a picture I would assume the people in it were all dead. I found myself thinking, about almost any project: "What's the point? I'll be dead before I can finish this."

I could shrug off that thought, I could get myself started but, for a time, it was my helpless, immediate impulse before any activity.

Of course, the great, unstoppable gift of Life is that there are other voices, other demands. And, as time passes, you can leave that airless cell of grief, if only to answer the other people who are pestering you.

Still, sorrow marks pastors, some more than others, but all to some degree. Towards the end of my service, I admitted to myself bluntly: I'm tired of human sorrow, I'm tired of seeing and hearing about suffering that will never be cured, that nobody can do anything about. If you said something like that out loud, your service would be over, you'd be useless from that point on. But I thought it, and I wanted it all to be done.

There was a family I liked a lot in the second church we served. Their oldest daughter had been a youth member on the committee that called us, when she was a high school senior. She was a happy, intelligent, pretty girl, with a great sense of community service. We got to know the family well, performed the weddings of the two oldest girls, had the younger son and daughter in confirmation, talked with all of them through the years about life, farming, schools, movies, jobs, kids, troubles. We felt at home in their kitchen.

The oldest daughter, now a teacher, and her husband had been trying to have a child and they finally succeeded. They were glowing, as new parents do, when they came back to visit with their new baby. It was one of the thrills of a long-term ministry to see kids grow up and start their own careers, families. It was nice to see.

A few weeks before we retired, her mother was delivering something at the church and hung around a bit to talk. She was easy to talk to and was also a movie fan, so I enjoyed running into her. She talked and talked and then finally brought out the thing that was making her talk. Her daughter had noticed she was having trouble getting her baby's attention and the doctors had just told them the baby was completely blind. There was something given or not given at birth, like the wrong card turning up in an unforgiving game.

The mother said, as we all do, to reach for comfort, to stop ourselves thinking, "You know, that baby's world hasn't changed one bit—he can't feel he's lost anything."

Neither of us had to spell out anything else.

You can tell me other people have the same grief or worse, much worse. You can tell me that this young couple—white Americans, with their own health, financially pretty secure—are still luckier than a lot of people. You won't be telling me anything I don't know. I can give you examples.

But every so often something will remind me of that bright young girl I met years ago, the way she looked with her new baby, and I will stop in my tracks as though I've been physically hit. I think the only reason I don't scream and scream and scream is that I already know, from experience, how pointless that would be.

Fade Out

One of the people we went to seminary with served his entire ministry in one parish. Another moved about every two years. We had two long-term periods of service, both in rural Minnesota: one on the Canadian border for almost sixteen years, and another about one-hundred-fifty miles northwest of Minneapolis for about twelve years.

Those years were hard on rural communities: farms getting larger and larger with fewer families on them; the creameries, the hardware stores, the clothing stores, the grocery stores, closing one after another; the schools consolidating, fighting about which buildings to close in which communities; church communities shrinking, aging. Those little towns could become angry places.

Certainly, the last town we served in, for whatever reason, did. People wanted the lives they had, or thought they had, or thought their parents had, back again. They fought more and more because they had less and less. No one would say anything as crazy as "Well, if we had a different football coach, co-op manager, school principal, or pastor, this town would be growing," but a lot of people acted as though they believed something like that. (Now that I think about it, I did hear that said once or twice.)

I wouldn't say I was burned out when I left. I certainly wasn't even close to a nervous breakdown. But I was definitely burned. I remarked to several people that I was through with the human race. To some I would add: it can tear itself apart without me.

I guess that does sound a little disturbed.

But I would find myself still mentally arguing with people, giving lectures about conflict, muttering, stabbing the air with my finger. Riding a train once, my wife tapped my arm and said, "You know, you look crazy when you're doing that." (And this was after we had been retired for a year.)

I imagined getting an invitation to come back for a parish anniversary. My reply would be short: "You couldn't get me back there with a gun to my head." I kept hoping for a chance to send it. I hoped people would ask

Fade Out

me to sum up what being a pastor was like in one word, and I would say: "Thankless."

Retired, I was set on avoiding extensive commitments. I found it very hard to be around people at first, except in very casual settings—like ordering a burger at a fast-food place. That was actually enough human contact for me for a week. I'm better now, but I find that I'm still happiest when I'm alone.

In Philip Roth's great novel *Sabbath's Theater*, he has his main character, Mickey Sabbath, reflect on how stupid his life has been. He says he knows he's had a stupid life *because there is no other kind.*

I'll put a Christian spin on that as I fade out.

If you turn over the parables and sayings of Jesus long enough, as I have for most of my life, it's hard to miss a dark undercurrent in them that might almost be called nihilism but never is because it's surrounded by so much light coming from elsewhere. Still, there's a sweeping dismissal, a scorn, of the things most of us spend most of our lives chasing.

Read the beatitudes (Matthew 5:1–13) seriously, not as an exercise in piety, but as a sober statement of who Jesus thinks is blessed, happy, fortunate, or lucky on earth and who isn't. Try not to laugh. The beatitudes reveal a completely different world of value than the one we live in ordinarily.

But the negative judgment in them is this: nothing that you think is important matters at all, nothing; all of the trophies and achievements and satisfactions and successes you measure your life by are meaningless; human goals are just as stupid as Mickey Sabbath says they are.

Jesus told a story once (Luke 16:1–13) that all preachers and most Christians puzzle over, at least in our time, a story that's easier for non-Christians to like. It's about an estate manager who's getting fired and is too lazy to get a job anywhere else. So he doctors all the estate accounts to let all the debtors of his master off the hook, thinking he'll make himself a lot of friends, his own golden parachute.

Here's what upsets all the Christians: Jesus doesn't tell us that the manager's wrong: he tells us to be more like him.

It's fun to listen to preachers twist and turn with this, so they don't sound like they're telling people cheating is OK. I twisted and turned a lot, too, until I figured out the problem.

Here it is: we all have tremendous respect for money, property, ownership, and the values of the world of money: honesty, hard work, accurate accounting. We respect this world without question or thought. Jesus not

All Hands Stand By to Repel Boarders

only doesn't respect it: he has contempt for it. How much we wrestle with that parable is a measure of how far we are from the way Jesus sees the world.

Our life is stupid. The things we chase in it and the things we measure it by are stupid.

It's all the stuff you can't work for or buy or steal, the stuff you don't get medals for having, the stuff that comes upon you once you give up on the garbage, that matters: joy, peace, patience, kindness, generosity, and all those other gifts we sing about so we don't have to believe in them or receive them.

But the Christian faith started in a graveyard, remember. It begins after the death of all the stupidity.

Here's the one real question: does that sound like salvation to you?

And, with that, I'll fade out . . .

Appendix to "Saint Ken"

Gospel text: John 6:51–58

(Note: Zion Lutheran was one of the churches my spouse and I were serving at this time; "Phil" was Ken's Music Director.)

EVERY TIME I IMAGINED getting up here, over the last couple of days, the first words that would come to my mind were: "Oh, Lord, why isn't Ken here?"

I never could think of a better way to start, so I guess that's what I really wanted to say. (And, to tell you the absolute truth, that's *all* I really wanted to say.) "Oh, Lord, why isn't Ken here?"

The Lord is probably used to hearing that from me, probably *sick* of hearing that from me. Usually—over the past 15 years—it's been in the form of "Why isn't Ken here to tell me what to do?" or "Why isn't Ken here so I can check this out with him before I do it?"

But today it's not the puzzles of pastoral tactics that prompt the question but the heart's lament. We know why Ken's not here. It's that deeper, bottomless *why?* that rises out of our grief and confusion, that outcry for sense and order, that desperate human longing that our treasures of flesh and blood might somehow defy their nature. "Oh, why, Lord?" It hardly counts as a question, no more than the wail of a child. And, anyway, no one's ever been given much of an answer.

It was about fifteen years ago that I first met Ken—which is a long time in *my* life (since I've lived here now longer than I've lived anywhere). But we'd just come up here and I was unpacking boxes alone one day and I heard this rap on the door. Well, I was hip deep in packing paper, furniture pads, books, plates, table legs, toys, dog dishes, objects I couldn't identify or remember owning, so it took me a second or two to get to the door—and he was already walking away. I thought: "Boy, not the most patient guy here." But I hailed him down and I can still see him in his casual clothes, turning

All Hands Stand By to Repel Boarders

with an eyebrow raised and his old pipe in his teeth and I could see he was thinking: "Is this new guy half-deaf or just slow?"

He introduced himself anyway and we discovered we were both from Chicago—and don't let him fool you about coming from this Tough City: he's from the *north side:* that's where the wimps live! (That's where the Cubs play!)—those guys have fondue parties and subscribe to *House Beautiful. I'm* from the tough part, the south side. We work in steel mills and if anything beautiful comes along, we smash it, right now.

Still, it was a bond, of sorts, up here, and after listening to a few of his wisecracks and wised-up assessments of the world, I knew he would be the perfect companion. (I told him this last week.) What I couldn't know, that first day, was that I had just met the best pastor I would ever see.

I wanted to go on, when I was writing this yesterday, and tell you he is also one of the most bull-headed drivers I've ever seen, most immune to helpful advice from the person quaking in the passenger seat—once, after we'd been lost for an hour on one of his shortcuts, I finally asked him where *he* thought the sun set: in the west or the east?

And then I wanted to talk about how he was the person I most wanted to see walk in the door when the world was collapsing around me. And about how many other people I've heard say that.

But I was afraid they might be recording this, and that he might hear it some day, and—since he is the best pastor I've ever seen—he would probably be saying about now: "Isn't it about time that this so-called preacher got around to the gospel?" (I can see him shaking his head and hear him going "Jeez!")

So I'll reach back instead to the oldest memory that we shared, the bond we had before his knuckles rapped on my door, the thing that brought Ken here, that brought me here, that brings us together here today, that binds us all beneath distance, the mind's quandaries, beneath the failures of the flesh and the gaping of the unknown: the bond of faith in Jesus Christ and his cross, the humanly senseless sign, at once defeat and victory, the gift to the baptized, and the way to the life of God.

Jesus said: "I am the living bread that came down from heaven. Whoever eats of this bread will live forever; and the bread that I will give for the life of the world is my flesh."

His sacrifice, his supper, the life he offers—it's all there.

And whenever I hear or read these words—"I am the living bread," "I am the bread of life"—I feel I've touched the center of all things, I'm at

Appendix to "Saint Ken"

the truth. They seem to glow with the kind of quiet power that silences everything around them.

And if I let them grip me, I can feel it descend on me—a quietness and a calm, an assurance and a peace. Here is the clear, central truth, whatever whirlwinds are roaring around me. This is the man I need, for nourishment, for life.

Jesus—the living bread come down from heaven: something clear as crystal, clear as a purely pitched bell on the stillest night.

For us, for believers, it has the simplicity and clarity of simple addition in math, or nursery rhymes. It's been with us all our days, it's just there, like the sun and the moon. It seems like a spotless pearl of divine wisdom, untainted by earth.

But Jesus spoke these words in the middle of a blazing argument—and not just a debate about taxes but one of those nasty, personal brawls along the lines of "Who do you think *you* are?"—because it's about who he is, and who we are, and what *life* is, and if there is hope.

And it does bear the taint of earth, as much as Jesus himself does, from the mess of being a human baby, to the bleeding and screaming of being nailed to a cross. The living bread come *down* from heaven—that "down" is important: down here, now, among us, for us, down here in the grief and confusion and senselessness and disorder of flesh and blood.

And how dare he say he can change that?

Here, of all places, we believers know instinctively that we must take what he says as a mystery, that we have to leap from the literal world of bread or the literal world of water to the signs of communion and baptism, that he is presenting heaven to us, offering eternal life to us, in the only way he can: through the signs of earth, but *as* signs of God's life.

Now, Jesus himself could argue pretty shrewdly when he wanted to but, if you read through chapter 6 in John, you don't see that. He simply restates what he's said already, as though he could not—at this most central point—figure out a way to break through. (This beautiful statement is in a chapter of arguments and fury.)

I would put it this way: we see heaven and earth staring at one another and neither side wants to budge. And what's standing between them is death (and all of death's shadows).

And then, all the anger and confusion and questions of the crowd (which, if you read on, led some people to turn away from Jesus) I would rephrase this way: "How *can* we believe what you say? Yes, our ancestors ate the bread in the wilderness and died—and so will we, no matter what we do. Don't tell us you can solve our problems because we know you can't—not the ones we want solved."

He can't argue with them because at this point you either go on with him in faith or you don't.

They're laying before him all the rage of the earth at its own powerlessness and finitude. And that rage is never very far from us, the rage of the creature at mortality and weakness, at the pointless blows of chance. It's easy to glare at heaven mercilessly, and there's always a lot to glare about—if not for you, then for your neighbor. It's always easy to hold court against God.

But heaven looks at us most clearly through this man Jesus, who shared our flesh and blood, who shared our death—and it's a look of mercy, with a promise of life.

But: we only receive it through faith, and sometimes that faith has to be held in the teeth of everything else we know.

One of Ken's favorite stories was about a pastor who rose at a funeral and said: "I have the duty of proclaiming to you today something I find it hard to believe." He told that story to me a lot, over the years, when some of you have suffered terrible tragedies and crushing grief.

But he did that duty faithfully. Because he did know, at just those times, you either go on in faith or you go nowhere.

Every time we speak the promise of Christ in this world we speak it in the face of the earth's rage at the truth it can see: suffering, hopelessness, death. There isn't an hour we worship or a minute we pray when someone, somewhere, isn't being crushed.

But this is what we live by, this is what Jesus is about: come *down* from heaven, into the sweat and blood and pain of life. We live by this—we go through suffering by this, and we die by this. If it was just for the times of sunshine and sweetness, why would we even bother to pay the water bill? It's not a matter of praising God when everything's rosy. We have to do this: this is the way to life.

We're all in a time of ignorance now, when the future is as dark as a pit. We're always tempted to light it for ourselves, one way or another. We send out flares of speculation and think we're seeing something. But we have those hard, elemental tasks, that become harder the purer that they are, unmixed with useful things to do and ironclad schedules to keep, and progress charts we can follow step by step: the tasks of watching and praying, hoping in *the unseen*, waiting upon the Lord, going in the strength of

Appendix to "Saint Ken"

the Lord when we have none, being witnesses for Christ in a world that says he does no good, where we don't get the good we dearly want. We have the task of faith. Faith in its purity: when we know nothing and can do nothing.

We sometimes ask, when life shatters, "Where was God?" I don't always have an answer for that—and I've asked it myself. But what I'm always driven back to is that rock-bottom Christian truth: when God was among us in the flesh, God was on the cross. That's where God is. When times are good, it's hard to face the pain of that. When times are bad, it's hard to face the hope of that.

But if we ask ourselves where the light is in the future, what's around to light our future, to show the way through the darkness—why, Christians, we stare at it every week. The cross is our future—through its pain to its glory.

We were marked with it, on our brows, when we were baptized: "child of God, you have been sealed by the Holy Spirit and marked with the cross of Christ forever." The child baptized this morning is growing into a future we cannot imagine, and most of our lives have held enough grief and woe that, if it was all laid together and shown us at the start, it would have stopped our hearts in fear. None of us know what's waiting there. But we can declare that the cross of Christ will be present there. And at the last edge of the world's sorrow, we may not be able to promise healing but we can promise the sure presence of God.

And that's both a promise for us and a call to us: to be witnesses to that presence of God and the power of Christ at the edge of sorrow.

Over at Zion Lutheran, we had Vacation Bible School this week—and if you remember your VBS days, you know that we're always singing about the sunshine and the breeze, the flowers and the trees. When I wasn't tripping over little, two-foot-long people, I was stepping on seeds and pictures of puppies. And it felt pretty weird, early in the week, to be singing with them about joy and praise and thanksgiving while I was thinking about Ken in Fargo and trying to figure out when I could get down there. I felt like I was flashing in and out of parallel and utterly different universes.

But it soon came to me: Christians always are. Christians always are. We proclaim a kingdom that is not yet. We live in one world and belong to another. Paul says "rejoice in the Lord always, give thanks to God at all times"—and he means it. The children have the same life we do—and we're being called to the same faith they're being called to. They may not think what Paul says is hard. And we may not think what he says is serious. But it is hard, *and yet* he is serious. Rejoice in the Lord always— not for the sake of what we see: but in the name of Christ.

He said: I am the Living Bread that came down from heaven—and we can read that as a call to order: come *here*, this is the center, *this* will last.

I read these words in Ken's room last week, when Phil and I got down there, and we had communion, and I want to say—with my fearful faith, as my duty that I find hard, as my response to that call, as my witness in the face of everything that defeats me, that the life and peace of Christ was among us. It didn't stop our sorrow or make me not want to scream, but it keeps and guards us and sets us toward the life of God, whether we understand it or not.

And now may this peace of God which passes all understanding keep your hearts and minds through Jesus Christ our Lord. Amen.

Appendix to
"Looking Back on The Great Thing"

Readings: Isaiah 25:1–9; Psalm 23; Philippians 4:1–9; Matthew 22:1–14

Gospel Reading:

Once more Jesus spoke to them in parables, saying: "The kingdom of heaven may be compared to a king who gave a wedding banquet for his son. He sent his slaves to call those who had been invited to the wedding banquet, but they would not come. Again he sent other slaves, saying, 'Tell those who have been invited: Look, I have prepared my dinner, my oxen and my fat calves have been slaughtered, and everything is ready; come to the wedding banquet.' But they made light of it and went away, one to his farm, another to his business, while the rest seized his slaves, mistreated them, and killed them. The king was enraged. He sent his troops, destroyed those murderers, and burned their city. Then he said to his slaves, 'The wedding is ready, but those invited were not worthy. Go therefore into the main streets, and invite everyone you find to the wedding banquet.' Those slaves went out into the streets and gathered all whom they found, both good and bad; so the wedding hall was filled with guests. "But when the king came in to see the guests, he noticed a man there who was not wearing a wedding robe, and he said to him, 'Friend, how did you get in here without a wedding robe?' And he was speechless. Then the king said to the attendants, 'Bind him hand and foot, and throw him into the outer darkness, where there will be weeping and gnashing of teeth.' For many are called, but few are chosen."

All Hands Stand By to Repel Boarders

OK. Who planned this wedding?! Holy Guacamole! What a nightmare!

People murdered, a city torched—a whole city! Burned down! Yeah, I really want an invitation to this! Oh, yeah!

There's so brutal a dress code that some poor slob (*who didn't even want to be there, man!*) gets tied up and tossed into . . . *the outer darkness* (whatever that is!). And that cold, cold judgement: "those invited were not worthy."

This is the worst wedding in the history of the universe!

We didn't come here to listen to this! We get bad news from everybody else! Lots of it! If we want to hear bad news, we'll watch CNN. If I want to hear bad news from my blood pressure, I'll watch FOX! We come *here* for the good news! The gospel! *Evangelium!* The happy message!

And we get—this? The kingdom of heaven *may be compared* to—this . . . mayhem? This carnage? This slaughter?

I want to talk about something else.

We have such beautiful readings today from Isaiah and Paul, words that for many of us are touchstones of promise. That wonderful feast in Isaiah of rich food and well-aged wines—the KJV translated that as "a feast of fat things"—mmm, you can taste the meat drippings!—the feast on the mountain where God will destroy the shroud of death and wipe away the tears from all faces: it takes us to the heart of human yearning.

And just as wonderful: St. Paul's summons to rejoice, rejoice *always*. Peaceful words to lead us to peace and gentleness. Promise and guidance together. The nearness of God and the needlessness of worry.

I think of Paul's closing admonition—to think about whatever's true, honorable, pleasing, any excellence—I think of that as the charter of Christian humanism: the generous, open-minded, open-hearted will to find all the goodness we can in life, and dwell on it and with it.

And those are just today's offerings! The Christian memory can call up a truckload of comfort and joy—words from Jesus himself: "Come to me, all you who are weary and heavy-laden and I will give you rest"; "Let not your hearts be troubled . . . in my father's house are many mansions: I go to prepare a place for you." Then there's everybody's favorite: Psalm 23—"Yea, though I walk through the valley of the shadow of death, I will fear no evil, for you are with me, your rod and your staff they comfort me." Me, me—not just everybody, not just anybody, *me*: that zoom-in to my sorrow, my trouble, my need, my life. *You*, Lord, comfort *me*.

Appendix to "Looking Back on The Great Thing"

Well, now we're talkin'! Now we're talkin'! All that blessed assurance, that amplitude of benevolent bounty, *sounds* the way we *expect JESUS* to sound. That's the kind of thing *I* want to hear! Is that the kind of thing *you* want to hear? You bet it is! *That's* what we want!

But now . . . now: did your mama ever tell you: "You can't have everything you want on this earth just because you want it"? Did you ever hear that? I heard it. I heard it a lot.

Suppose we ask: Who is this God that Isaiah and Paul talk about, who is this shepherd that makes us feel so safe, so good?

Well, if God can deliver this truckload of comfort and consolation in the teeth of the world's fury, in the valley of the shadow of death itself, then somewhere inside the God of promise, the God of protection and peace, there is the God of power: you can hear the power humming underneath the confidence, the trust, the joy. The majesty and the power *guarantee* the love.

Paul is in prison when he writes *Philippians*. Why's he so peaceful? Because Paul got to a place of the spirit where the powers of the earth, the rewards of the earth, the pains and the pleasures of the earth, were nothing, *nothing, NOTHING* compared to the greatness and the power of God.

Look: Isaiah spells it out for us: why is everything so peaceful on that holy mountain? There's nothing else left. God destroyed all disgrace and danger, up to and including death. But *up to*—how about verse 2: "you have made the city a heap . . . the palace of aliens is no more; it will never be rebuilt." This is scorched earth, an image taken from war. We know pretty well what heaps of rubble in cities look like after an attack. It's not pretty.

So, in this beautiful, comforting passage, we have *another city destroyed* in the run-up *to the feast* at the end of the world: for all the difference in tone, when you look deeper, Isaiah and Matthew are a little too close for comfort. Maybe we should take another look at that horrific parable . . .

Who usually gets invited to a wedding? The invitations tend to trace the lives of the bride and groom—family, friends, maybe people from work, maybe friends of friends. They're not all people the bride and groom would die for, but there's some relationship there, some connection. The guest list reflects who the couple is.

We all *know* that, but we really *feel* it when we don't get an invitation we expect: you feel a judgment about your relationship: it's different than what you thought it was.

But the essential point is: a *wedding* party is about something deeper: our place in each other's lives. Also: unless it's your wedding, what that place *is* is not up to you.

Something like that is true at the start of Jesus' parable. The invitations *were out*—assume they didn't go to everybody. There are established relationships here. Since we're talking about the kingdom of God, we begin with those who in some explicit way can be considered the people of God, the community of faith. It's not about everybody in general but about believers.

The detonator that sets off the parable is this: the people close enough to the king to rate an invitation, those invited, *won't come*. That's a judgment on the relationship from the other side. It's like when an invitation you send gets tossed in the garbage.

Jesus is telling us something about God and something about the people of God. And, first off, notice this: here's a king who goes the extra mile: he sends out another wave of servants, spells out all the preparations, stresses the urgency—mmmmm, can't you just smell those fat calves roasting? *It means, we're starting here: let's move.*

"But they made *light of it* and went away."

Hang on to the phrase ("made light of it") because I think that's really Jesus' fundamental indictment of the believing community. This parable has an impact because of its violence, violence on both sides. But the violence of the invited guests—when some of them kill the king's messengers—is only an extreme instance of a broader and sometimes more hidden rejection: they *made light of it*—it didn't mean anything to them, *it was no big deal.* It's a subtle corruption at the heart of the easy religious life: it's not that serious, it doesn't matter *that much.*

One goes to his farm, another to his business: those aren't evil things, that's just normal life. Say more than that: those are excuses we *accept.* (You want to know how many times I've heard them?) "Hey, I'd like to come but I gotta work." Or how about putting it this way: "I can't do this because it might cost me my job." Or: "I should report this, but I might lose my job." Acceptable excuse for skipping a lot. When does it stop being acceptable—either on earth or before heaven?

Let's say Jesus wants to get us worrying about that question.

Now, just that far in the parable, we still have a fairly realistic comparison. Once the violence starts, we are in a nightmare, a horror story, brutal, unforgiving. And it's the rage and violence *of the king* that's so unnerving.

Appendix to "Looking Back on The Great Thing"

The rage seems total and disproportionate: the king goes after everybody that turned him down: murderously or not. Remember: some went back to business, some to farm. It's the mere fact of refusing the invitation that gets them killed, gets their city burned down.

But most unnerving of all: Jesus is seriously presenting this as an image of God's kingdom, who God is, God's intent *now* towards God's own people.

We could say the violence is a measure of the seriousness of the call, the seriousness of faith. I think that would be true, but I also think it's a little off target.

In this less and less realistic story, the king's rage *and his invitation of others* show one thing: this banquet is about what God wants: it's not first about you or me or anybody in particular: it's about what God wants. Sure, people get invited, God does want a community of faith celebrating, but don't be fooled: with or without you, this banquet is going to happen—in the end, it's not about you but the banquet, the gathering God wants to happen. And it will.

That wedding hall fills up. That's the promise: this is a story about the relentless determination of God. This *is* the God that sets that feast on the holy mountain, this *is* the God that enters the valley of the shadow of death with saving power, the God that will not be stopped.

The hall is filled with guests, both good and bad, the ordinary human mix—it could be a picture of the church in any age, a picture of us.

∽ ∽ ∽

But the story's not over—and this is where Jesus sticks in the knife. (I love this part.)

Everything's been on a large scale: mass invitations, gangs of servants, mass destruction, random gathering of a crowd: now the king stoops to *one*. God comes down, face to face. Another zoom-in.

We treasure that personal look, that zoom-in to my life in the passage of comfort: *you* spread a table before *me*; Jesus saying "Come to *me*, *you* who are weary," "I go to prepare a place for *you*."

But would we always welcome that visitation?

You, Lord, look at *me*.

"Friend, how'd *you* get in here without a wedding robe?"

Look: this robeless sap isn't said to be one of "the bad." I'll bet he's speechless! He got dragged in! But he took being there lightly—in some

215

other way than the first guys. Something that ought to unnerve us further, as Jesus isn't that specific about what that way was.

Except that it will get us thrown into the outer darkness, where there's weeping and gnashing of teeth.

There have been many things said, over the centuries, to soften this parable. I've heard the man without the robe identified as Judas—not me, not you: don't worry about it. I've heard the robe identified as the robe of righteousness, the garment of baptism—I have that, so have you: don't worry about it. It's ridiculously easy for preachers to stand up and scream about . . . somebody else's sin: they *better* worry. (Not me, not you.)

But once we soften it or deflect it, we're not listening anymore. Every detail in the story drags us face to face with that threat of expulsion into outer darkness. I think Jesus doesn't get specific at the end because his whole point *is* for us to tremble, to stay worried. Or better yet: stay *mindful* of the one power, one power, we have to bow to, attend to, one power, *period*.

That *is* good news. Sometimes the harshest words are the greatest gifts, the words that give us a spine, that wake us up to the fact that we're not the center of the universe: God is. We should let Jesus tell us brutally that we're invited to God's kingdom, so we should act like it. We should let Jesus leave us troubled about what that means.

I have a set of devotional books that gather readings and prayers from all the Christian centuries, and I once found in it an inscription taken from the cathedral in Lubeck, Germany, that I thought summed up this passage. So I'm going to end with it:

> Thus speaketh Christ our Lord to us:
> Ye call me Master, and obey me not;
> Ye call me Light, and see me not;
> Ye call me Way, and walk me not;
>
> Ye call me Life, and desire me not;
> Ye call me Wise, and follow me not,
> Ye call me Fair, and love me not;
> Ye call me Rich, and ask me not;
>
> Ye call me Eternal, and seek me not;
> Ye call me Gracious, and trust me not;
> Ye call me Noble, and serve me not;
> Ye call me Mighty, and honor me not;

Appendix to "Looking Back on The Great Thing"

> Ye call me Just, and fear me not;
> If I condemn ye, blame me not.

And that *is* the good news this morning!
Amen.

www.ingramcontent.com/pod-product-compliance
Lightning Source LLC
Chambersburg PA
CBHW070313230426
43663CB00011B/2109